Learning the Arabic language: Level 1

تَعَلُّمُ اللُّغَةِ العَرَبِيَّةِ: الْمُسْتَوَى الأَوَّل

A beginner's journey into the Arabic language

رِحْلَةُ الْمُبْتَدِئِينَ فِي تَعَلُّمِ اللُّغَةِ العَرَبِيَّةِ

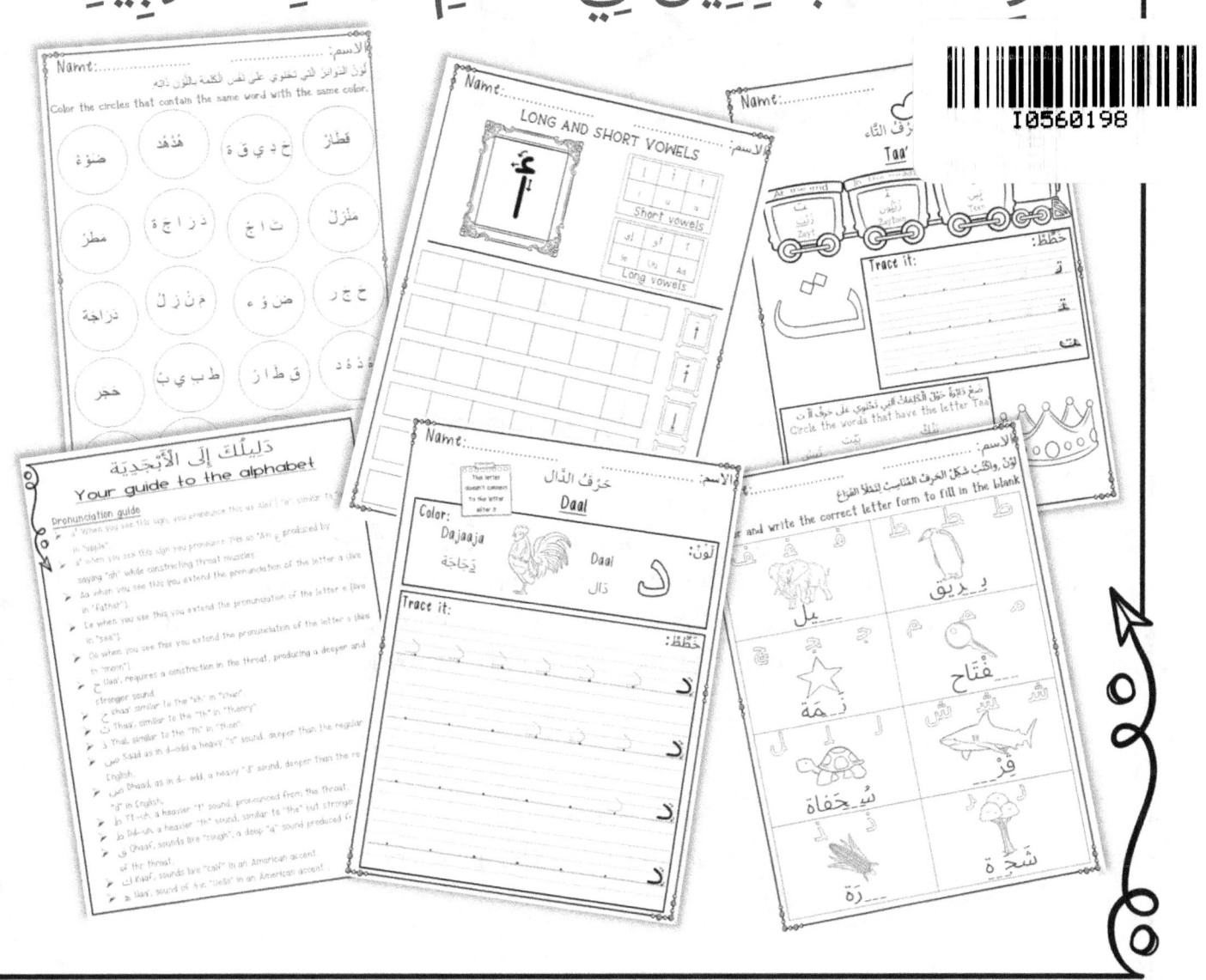

Table of contents

Table of contents

This book belongs to:

_____

مُقَدِّمَة لِلْحُرُوفِ ٱلْعَرَبِيَّةِ
Introduction to the alphabet

- The Arabic language is written from right to left.

  اللُّغَةُ الْعَرَبِيَّةُ تُكْتَبُ مِنَ الْيَمِينِ إِلَى الْيَسَارِ.

- In Arabic, most letters within a word are connected, resembling handwriting.

  فِي اللُّغَةِ الْعَرَبِيَّةِ، يَتَّصِلُ مُعْظَمُ الْحُرُوفِ فِي الْكَلِمَةِ بِطَرِيقَةٍ تُشْبِهُ الْكِتَابَةَ الْيَدَوِيَّةَ.

- Certain letters do not connect to the next letter due to their shape.

  بَعْضُ الْحُرُوفِ لَا تَتَّصِلُ بِالْحَرْفِ الَّذِي يَلِيهَا بِسَبَبِ شَكْلِهَا.

- The Arabic alphabet consists of 28 letters.

  الْأَبْجَدِيَّةُ الْعَرَبِيَّةُ تَتَأَلَّفُ مِنْ 28 حَرْفًا.

- There is no such thing as capital and small letters.

  لَا يُوجَدُ فِي اللُّغَةِ الْعَرَبِيَّةِ حُرُوفٌ كَبِيرَةٌ وَصَغِيرَةٌ.

- Vowels are represented by separate marks placed above or below the letters.

  الْحَرَكَاتُ تُمَثَّلُ بِعَلَامَاتٍ مُنْفَصِلَةٍ تُوضَعُ أَعْلَى أَوْ أَسْفَلَ الْحَرْف.

- Each letter of the Arabic alphabet has a unique shape and sound and it can transform into four similar forms:

  كُلُّ حَرْفٍ مِنْ حُرُوفِ الْأَبْجَدِيَّةِ الْعَرَبِيَّةِ لَهُ شَكْلٌ وَصَوْتٌ مُمَيَّزٌ، وَيُمْكِنُ أَنْ يَظْهَرَ بِأَرْبَعَةِ أَشْكَالٍ مُتَشَابِهَةٍ:

- By itself   بِمُفْرَدِهِ
- In the beginning of a word   فِي بِدَايَةِ الْكَلِمَةِ
- In the middle of a word   فِي مُنْتَصَفِ الْكَلِمَةِ
- At the end of a word   فِي نِهَايَةِ الْكَلِمَةِ

مُقَدِّمَة لِلْحُرُوف ٱلْعَرَبِيَّة
Introduction to the alphabet

*Here's an example: :
The letter Taa (ت) has 4 forms

*إِلَيْكُمْ مِثَالاً:
حَرْفُ التَّاءِ لَهُ أَرْبَعَةُ أَشْكَالٍ

By itself	ت	بِمُفْرَدِه
In the beginning of a word	تـ	فِي بِدَايَةِ الْكَلِمَةِ
In the middle of a word	ـتـ	فِي مُنْتَصَفِ الْكَلِمَةِ
At the end of a word	ـت	فِي نِهَايَةِ الْكَلِمَةِ

*here's a list of the Arabic vowels

*إِلَيْكُمْ قَائِمَةٌ بِالْحَرَكَاتِ الْعَرَبِيَّةِ.

Kasra (E)	ِ	كَسْرَة
Fatha (A)	َ	فَتْحَة
Damma (U)	ُ	ضَمَّة
2 Kasra (EN)	ٍ	كَسْرَتَانْ
2 Fatha (AN)	ً	فَتْحَتَانْ
2 Dhamma (UN)	ٌ	ضَمَّتَانْ
Sukun	ْ	سُكُونْ
Shadda	ّ	شَدَّة
Waw (UU)	و	وَاو
Alif (AA)	ا	أَلِف
Yaa (EE)	ي	يَاءْ

8

دَلِيلُكَ إِلَى الأَبْجَدِيَة
Your guide to the alphabet

Pronunciation guide

➢ a' When you see this sign, you pronounce this as Alef أ "a", similar to "a" in "apple".

➢ a' when you see this sign you pronounce this as 'Ain ع produced by saying "ah" while constricting throat muscles.

➢ Aa when you see this you extend the pronunciation of the letter a (like in "father").

➢ Ee when you see this you extend the pronunciation of the letter e (like in "see").

➢ Oo when you see this you extend the pronunciation of the letter o (like in "moon").

➢ ح Haa', requires a constriction in the throat, producing a deeper and stronger sound.

➢ خ Khaa' similar to the "kh" in "khan".

➢ ث Thaa', similar to the "th" in "theory".

➢ ذ Thal, similar to the "th" in "then".

➢ ص Saad as in d—odd a heavy "s" sound, deeper than the regular "s" in English.

➢ ض Dhaad, as in d— odd, a heavy "d" sound, deeper than the regular "d" in English,

➢ ط Tt—uh, a heavier "t" sound, pronounced from the throat.

➢ ظ Dd—uh, a heavier "th" sound, similar to "the" but stronger.

➢ ق Qhaaf, sounds like "cough", a deep "q" sound produced from the back of thr throat.

➢ ك Kaaf, sounds like "calf" in an American accent.

➢ ه Haa', sound of *h* in "Hello" in an American accent .

دَلِيلُكَ إِلَى الأَبْجَدِيَة
Your guide to the alphabet

Short vowels guide:

➤ Short vowel in Arabic are called "Harakat"(حَرَكَات) which means "movements" , they give the letters their pronunciation.

➤ They are not a part of the alphabet; they are symbols written above or below the letters.

➤ These vowels are used to help you write and read words more easily, even if you don't know the word's meaning.

➤ These are the short vowels:

– Fatha " فَتْحَة " َ is a diagonal line above the letter. It make an "a" sound. For example,when Fatha is placed above the letter Baa' "ب", it produces the sound "Ba"بَ.

– Kasra " كَسْرَة " ِ is a diagonal line below the letter. It make an "i" sound. When Kasra is placed under the letter Baa' "ب" it produces the sound Bi بِ.

– Dhamma " ضَمّة " ُ is a small curl above the letter. It make an "u" sound. When Dhamma is placed above the letter Baa' "ب" it produces the sound Bu بُ.

Sukoon "سُكون" ْ

– Is a small circle written above the letter.

– Sukoon means "still" or "rest", it shows that the letter is not followed by a vowel sound—it's "silent".

– Indicate the absence of any vowel sounds, for example, the letter "بْ" is pronounced simple as "B".

دَلِيلُكَ إِلَى الْأَبْجَدِيَة
<u>Your guide to the alphabet</u>

<u>Tanween "تَنْوِين" means doubling the short vowels</u>

- Tanween is only placed on the last letter of the word
- Tanween is a combination of the sound "n" (from the letter "نْ" with a short vowel (example: ◌َ +نْ = ◌ً it sound like a "–an")
- Tanween with fatha is usually followed by an extra alif "أ" with 2 exceptions:

1. If the word ends with a ta marboota " ة " (example: وَرَقَةً)
2. If the word ends with a Hamza " ء " and the second–last letter is an " ا " (example: شِتَاءً)

- There are three types of Tanweens:
1. Tanween Fatha (Fathatain) " فَتْحَتان :" مُفْتَاحاً ← مُفْتَاحْ
2. Tanween Dhamma (dammatain) " ضَمَتَانْ : " قَلَمٌ ← قَلَمْ
3. Tanween Kasrah (Kasratayn) " كسرتين : " بَيْتٍ ← بَيْتْ

<u>Long vowels</u>

- Alif " أ ":
  - Its pronounced as "aa"
  - The letter before the Alif must have a fatha ◌َ
- Yaa' " ي ":
  - Its pronounced as "ii"
  - The letter before the yaa' must have a Kasra ◌ِ
- Waw " و ":
  - Its pronounced as " uu "
  - The letter before the waw must have a dhamma ◌ُ

دَليلُكَ إِلَى الأَبْجَدِيَّة
Your guide to the alphabet

Shadda " شَدَّة " ّ

- It resembles the letter "W" in the English alphabet
- Shadda replaces two identical consonants with one letter. For example, the word "Toffah" (تُفَّاحَة) has double "F" sound. In Arabic instead of writing تُفْفَاحَة we write تُفَّاحَة
- Shadda can only replace double letters when the first letter has a Sukoon and the second letter has a short vowel. For instace, in سَيْيَارَة the first "ي" has a Sukoon and the second "ي"one has vowel, which allows the second "ي" to be replaced by a Shadda سَيَّارَة

* Short vowels (fatha, dhamma, kasra) can be used with shadda:
- Fatha (◌َ) is placed above the shadda سُكَّر
- Dhamma (◌ُ) is placed above the shadda يُحِبُّ
- Kasra (◌ِ) is placed under the shadda not the letter مُعَلِّم

Ta marboota ة

- Ta marboota (ة) is the rounded form of the letter Taa " ت ".

It can appear in two forms (ة or ـة) depending on whether the previous letter connects to other letters or not. Example: طَويلَة / قَصيرَ

- It can be pronounced in two ways:
  1. Pronounced as –at: and It appears at the end of:
  - Feminine proper noun فَاطِمَة
  - Feminine singular noun that does not have a masculine form طَاوِلَة
  - Some broken plurals أَسَاتِذَة
  - Some adjectives that are derived from a masculine form قَديمَة

دَلِيلُكَ إِلَى الأَبْجَدِية
Your guide to the alphabet

2. Pronounced as —ah:

- When a word ends in ta marboota ة and is followed by a pause or appears at the end of a sentence, it is pronounced as —ah. Example : ذَكِيَة is pronounced ذَكِيَه.

- When there is no short vowel or tanween on the ta marboota.

Hamza " ء " :

Hamza can appear in 4 ways:
- By itself on the line → ء
- On or under the letter Alif " ا " → إ/أ
- On the letter Yaa' " ي " → ئ
- On the letter waw " و " → ؤ

In Arabic, most letters connect to the letter after them, except for six letter: أ (Alif), د (Daal), ذ (Thaal), ر (Raa'), ز (Zayn) and و (Waw). These letters always appear disconnected from the letter after them.

الْحُرُوف الْعَرَبِيَّة
Arabic alphabets

ث	ت	ب	أ
Thaa'	Taa'	Baa'	Alif
ثَاء	تَاء	بَاء	أَلِف
د	خ	ح	ج
Daal	Khaa'	Haa'	Jeem
دَال	خَاء	حَاء	جِيم
س	ز	ر	ذ
Seen	Zayn	Raa'	Thaal
سِين	زَيْن	رَاء	ذَال
ط	ض	ص	ش
Taa'	Dhaad	Saad	Sheen
طَاء	ضَاد	صَاد	شِين
ف	غ	ع	ظ
Faa'	Ghain	'Ain	Zaa'
فَاء	غَيْن	عَيْن	ظَاء
م	ل	ك	ق
Meem	Laam	Kaaf	Qaaf
مِيم	لام	گَاف	قَاف
ي	و	ه	ن
Yaa'	Waaw	Ha'	Noon
يَاء	وَاو	هَاء	نُون

Name:........................ .... :الاسْم

حَرْفُ الأَلِف

Alif

This letter doesn't connect to the letter after it

Color: لَوِّنْ:

'Arnab
أَرْنَب

'Alif
أَلِف

أ

Trace it: خَطِّطْ:

This letter doesn't connect to the letter after it

حَرْفُ الأَلِف

Alif

| أ
خَطَأ
Khataa' | ا
بَاب
Baab | أ
أَرْنَب
Arnab |

Trace it: خَطِّط :

أ

ا

أَ

ضَعْ دَائِرَةْ حَوْلْ الْكَلِمَاتْ الَّتِي تَحْتَوِي عَلَى حَرْفِ الْ أ

Circle the words that have the letter Alif

قِرْد   أَسَد

وَرْدة

قَرَأَ   مُرَبَّع

دَجَاجَة   قَهْوة

بَدَأَ

أَنَانَاس   بَارِد

LONG AND SHORT VOWELS

This letter doesn't connect to the letter after it

اِ	اُ	اَ
i	u	a

Short vowels

إِي	أُو	آ
Ie	Uu	Aa

Long vowels

حَرْفُ البَاء

Baa'

Color: لَوِّنْ:

Batta   Baa'   **ب**

بَطَّة   بَاء

Trace it: خَطِّطْ:

ب

ب

ب

ب

حَرْفُ الْبَاء

Baa'

At the end	In the middle	In the beginning
ب	بْ	بَ
كَلْب	حَبْل	بَيْت
Kalb	Habl	Bayt

ب

Trace it:

خَطِّط:

بَ

بْ

ب

ضَعْ دَائِرَةْ حَوْلَ ٱلْكَلِمَاتْ ٱلتِي تَحْتَوِي عَلَى حَرِفْ ٱلـ ب

Circle the words that have the letter Baa'

أَزْرَق   بَطَّة   مُرَبَّع

دُب   بَقَرَة

هَاتِف   دِيك

أَخْطَبُوط   سَيَّارَة   حَاسُوب

Name:.....................   ....

LONG AND SHORT VOWELS

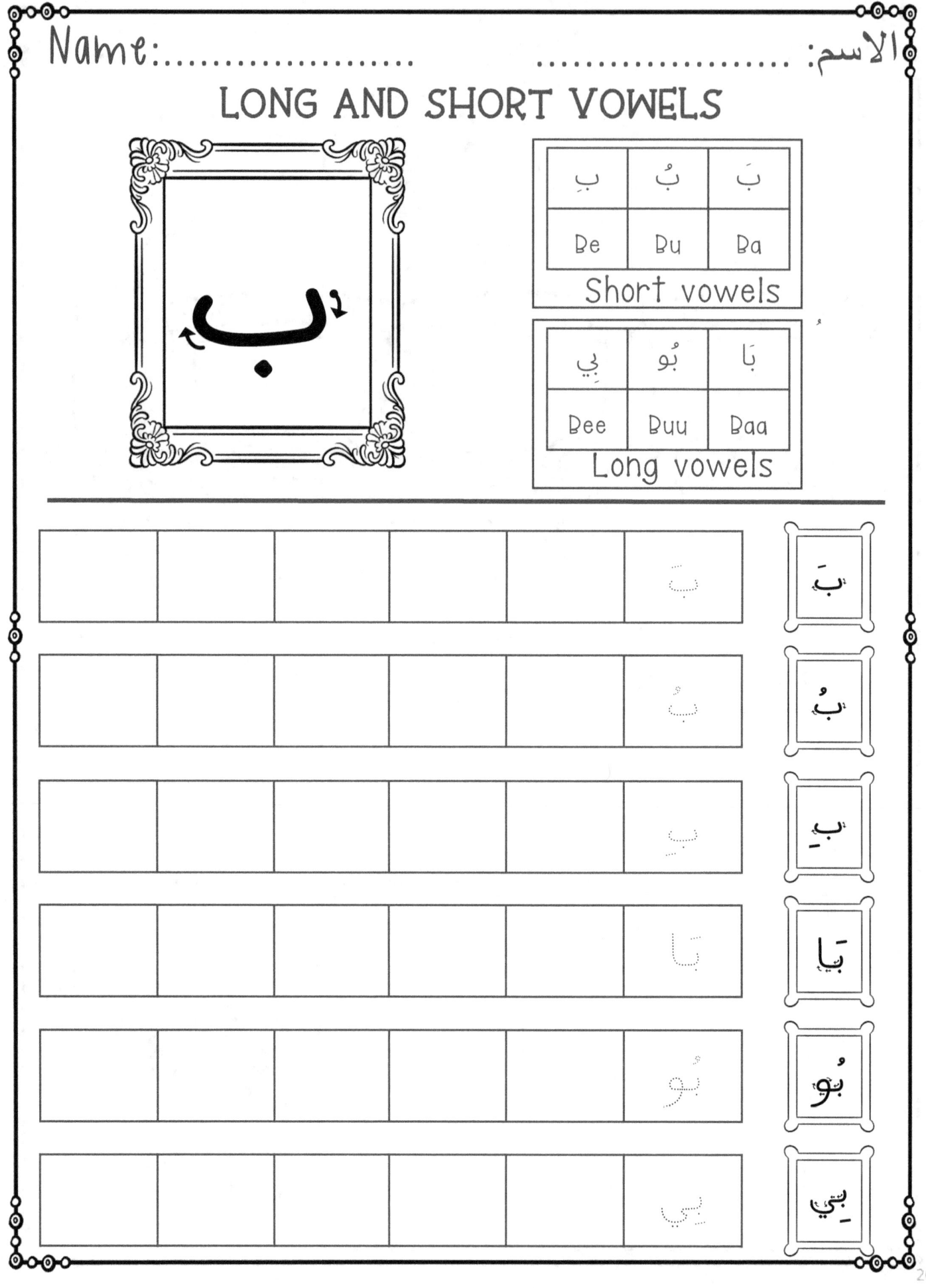

بِ	بُ	بَ
Be	Bu	Ba

Short vowels

بِي	بُو	بَا
Bee	Buu	Baa

Long vowels

حَرْفُ التَّاء

Taa'

لَوِّنْ:		Color:
ت		Tofaaha
تَاء Taa'		تُفَّاحَة

خَطِّظْ:   Trace it:

ت

ت

ت

ت

حَرْفُ التَّاء

Taa'

At the end	In the middle	In the beginning
ت	تـ	تـ
زَيْت	زَيْتُون	تِين
Zayt	Zaytoon	Teen

خَطِّطْ: **Trace it:**

ت
تـ
ـتـ

ضَعْ دَائِرَةً حَوْلَ ٱلْكَلِمَاتْ ٱلتِي تَحْتَوِي عَلَى حَرِفْ ٱلْ ت

Circle the words that have the letter Taa'

بَنْك	بَيْت	تَيْس
دُب	تَاج	
حُوت	بِنْت	
كُتُب	عَجِين	هَاتِف

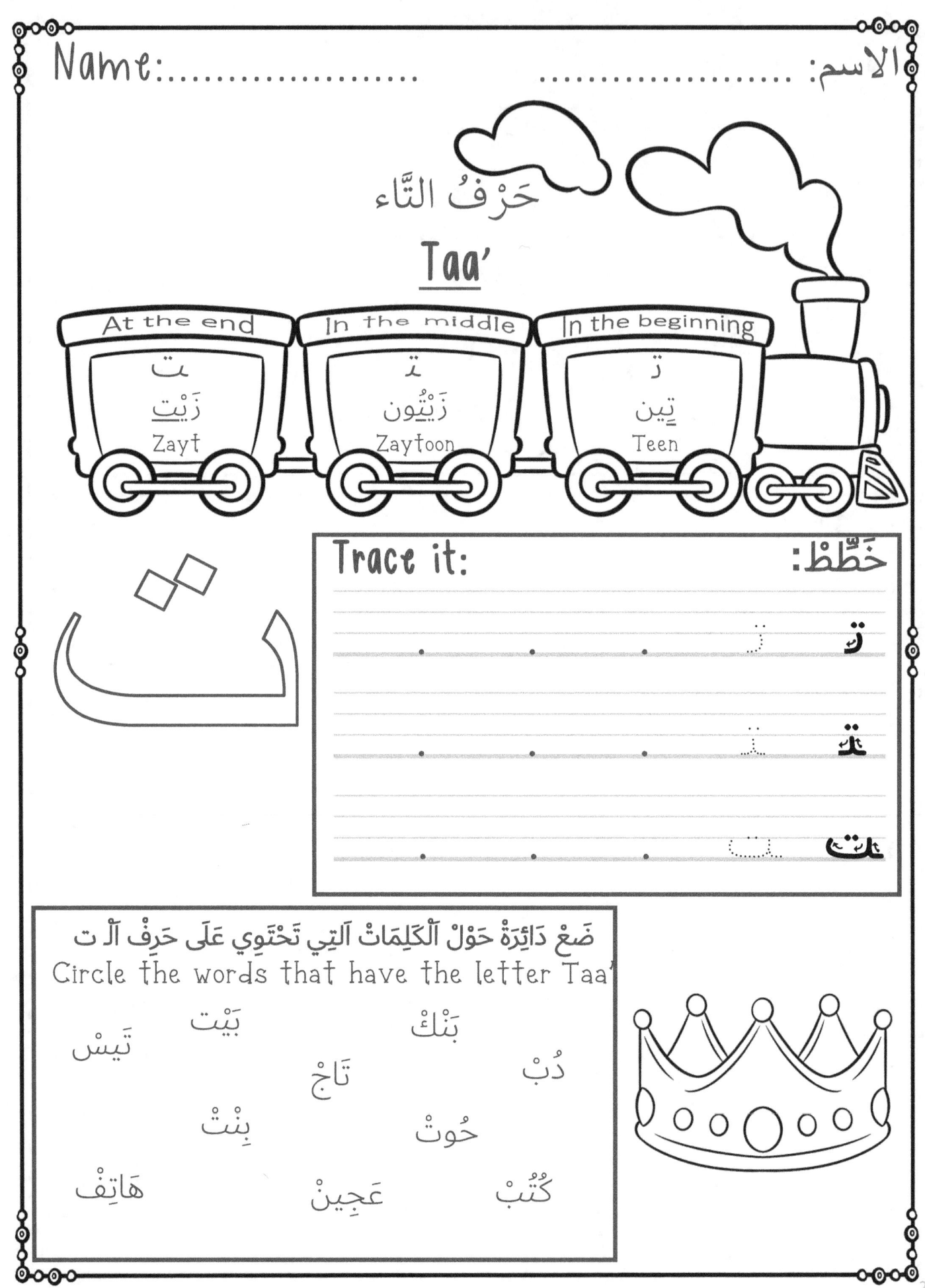

22

LONG AND SHORT VOWELS

تَ	تُ	تِ
Te	Tu	Ta

Short vowels

تِي	تُو	تَا
Tee	Tuu	Taa

Long vowels

حَرْفُ الثَّاء

Thaa'

Color:	:لَوِّنْ
Tha'lab	Thaa'
ثَعْلَب	ثَاء

ث

Trace it: خَطِّطْ:

ثـ

اثـ

ثـ

ث

Name:................................... .... :الاسم

حَرْفُ الثَّاء

Thaa'

At the end	In the middle	In the beginning
ث حَدِيث Hadith	ـثـ مُثَلَّجَات Mothalajat	ثـ ثَعْلَب Tha'lab

Trace it: خَطِّظ:

ثـ

ـثـ

ـث

ضَعْ دَائِرَةً حَوْلَ الْكَلِمَاتْ الّتِي تَحْتَوِي عَلَى حَرِفْ الْـ ث
Circle the words that have the letter Thaa'

	مُثَلَّث	ثَلَاثَة
غَيْث	حُب	دُودَة
مَوْز	ثَوْب	
ثَلِج	لَيْث	فِيل

25

LONG AND SHORT VOWELS

ثِ	ثُ	ثَ
The	Thu	Tha

Short vowels

ثِي	ثُو	ثَا
Thee	Thuu	Thaa

Long vowels

ثَ

ثُ

ثِ

ثَا

ثُو

ثِي

حَرْفُ الجِيم

Jeem

Color:			لَوِّنْ:

Jaras   Jeem

جَرَس   جَيم

Trace it:	خَطِّط:

حَرْفُ الجِيم

Jeem

At the end	In the middle	In the beginning
ـج	ـجـ	جـ
ثَلْج	شَجَرَة	جَمَل
Thalj	Shajara	Jamal

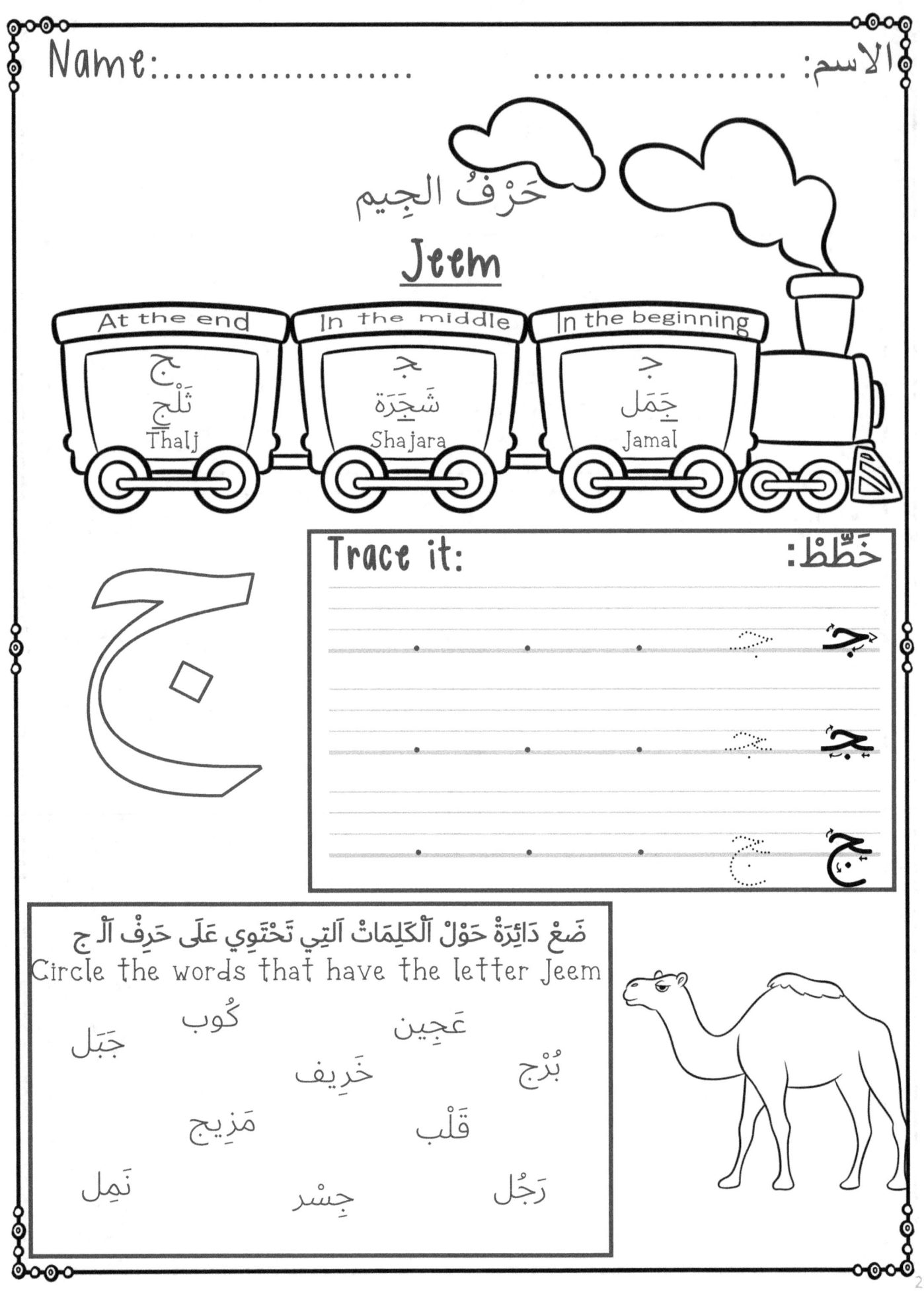

خَطِّط : Trace it:

جـ

يجـ

ـج

ضَعْ دَائِرَة حَوْلَ الْكَلِمَاتْ الِتِي تَحْتَوِي عَلَى حَرِفْ الْ ج
Circle the words that have the letter Jeem

كُوب   عَجِين

جَبَل   بُرْج

خَرِيف

مَزِيج   قَلْب

رَجُل

نَمِل   جِسْر

LONG AND SHORT VOWELS

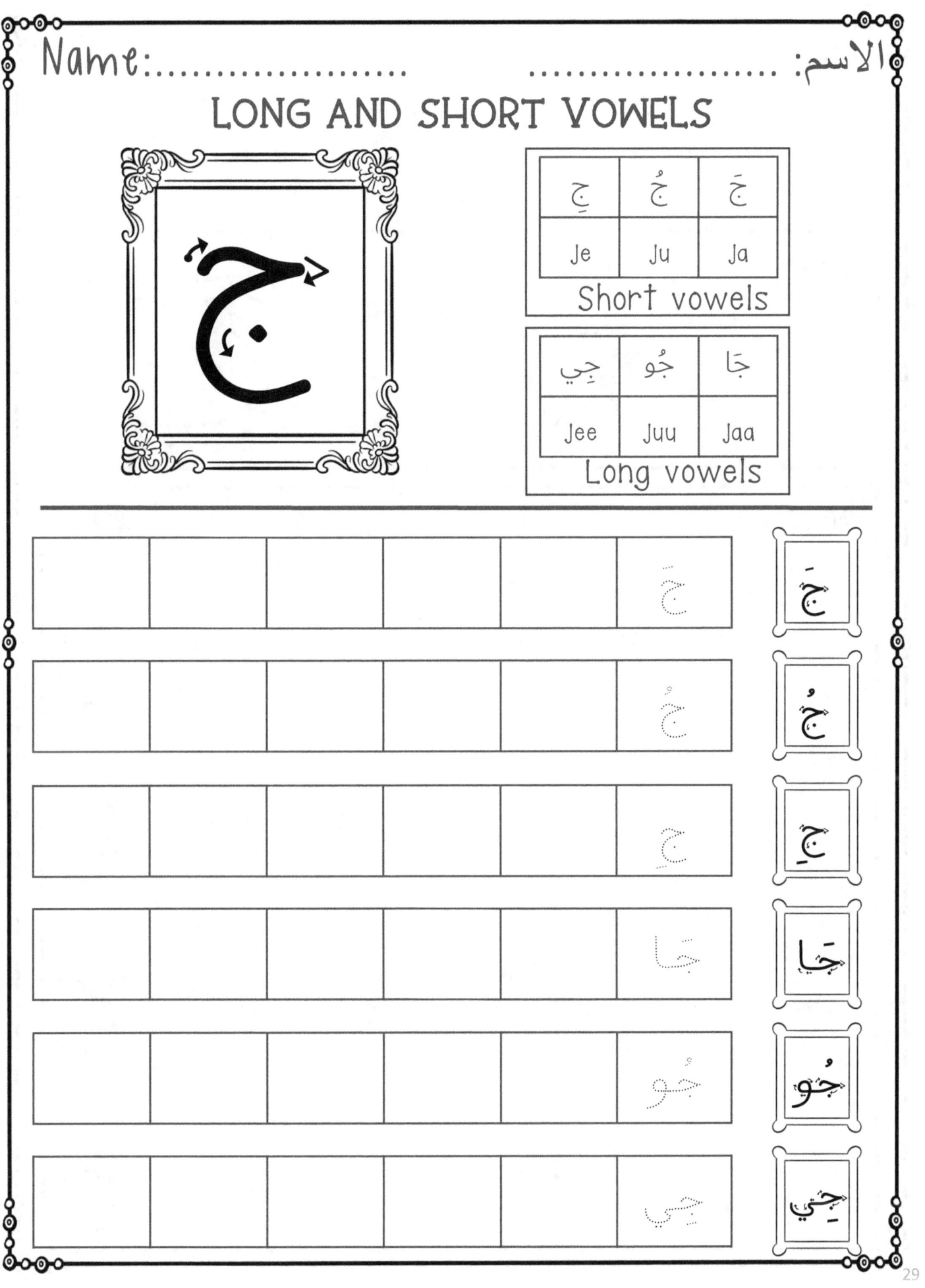

جِ	جُ	جَ
Je	Ju	Ja

Short vowels

جِي	جُو	جَا
Jee	Juu	Jaa

Long vowels

Name:................... .... :الاسم

حَرْفُ الْحَاءِ

Haa'

Color: لَوِّنْ:

Hoot   Haa'

حُوت   حَاء

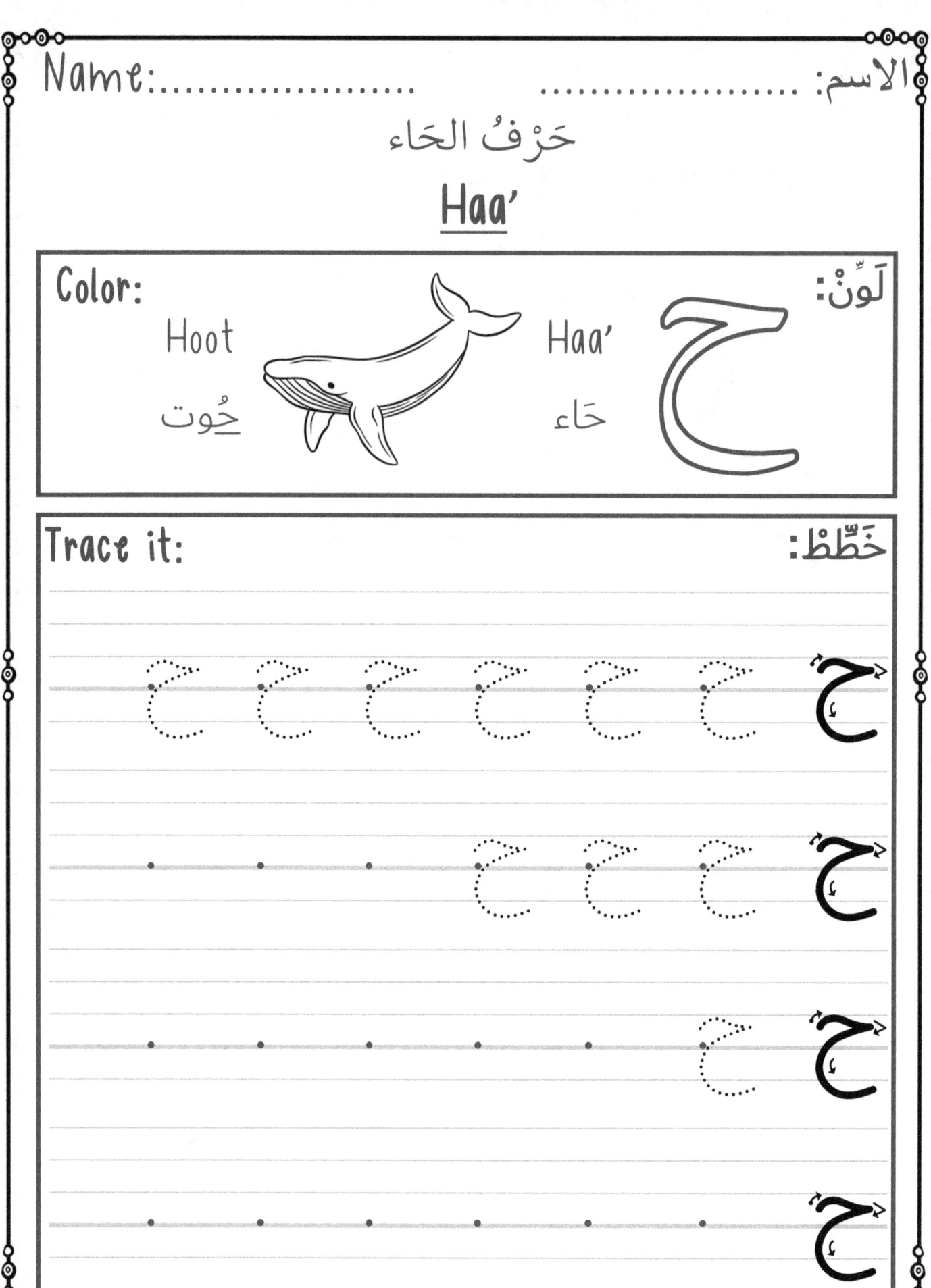

Trace it: خَطِّطْ:

ح

ح

ح

ح

حَرْفُ الحَاء

Haa'

At the end	In the middle	In the beginning
ح	ح	ح
مِلْح	بَحْر	حِصَان
Milh	Bahr	Hisan

Trace it: خَطّط:

ح

ح

ح

ضَعْ دَائِرَةْ حَوْلْ الْكَلِمَاتْ آلتِي تَحْتَوِي عَلَى حَرِفْ آلح

Circle the words that have the letter Haa'

نَحْلَة	حُبُوب	رَبِيع	
		لَحِم	
	مَاء		
قُبَّعَة		بَلَح	
أَسْوَد	حَمَامَة	قَمِح	

Name:................... .... :الاسم

LONG AND SHORT VOWELS

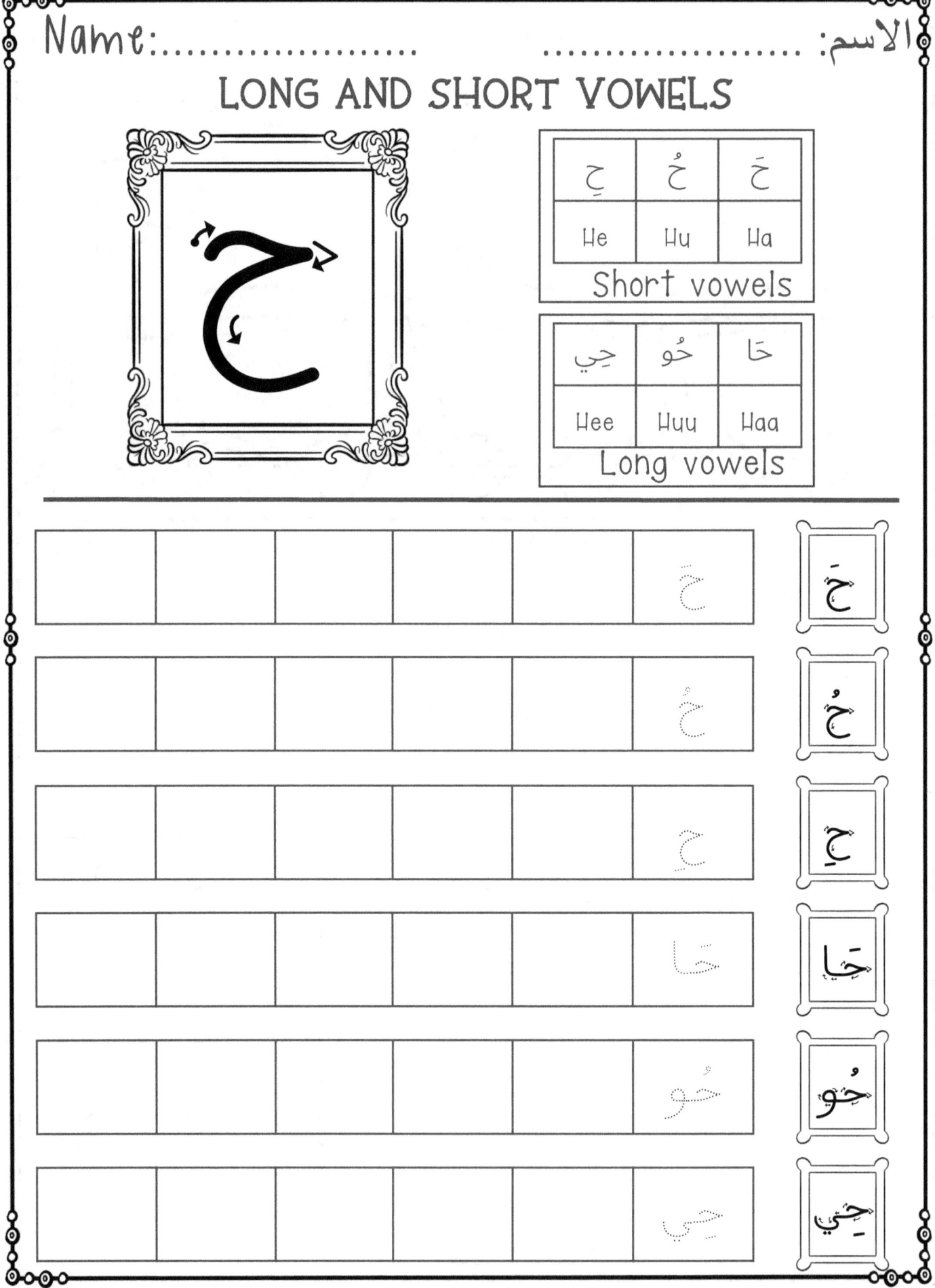

حِ	حُ	حَ
He	Hu	Ha

Short vowels

حَا حِي	حُو حِي	حَا
Hee	Huu	Haa

Long vowels

حَرْفُ الخَاء

<u>khaa'</u>

Color:		لَوِّنْ:

Khubz

خُبْز

khaa'

خَاء

خ

Trace it: خَطِّطْ:

ع ع ع ع ع ع   خِ

        ع ع ع   خُ

                ع   خِ

                                                    خِ

Name:................................ .... :الاسم

حَرْفُ الخَاء

Khaa'

At the end	In the middle	In the beginning
خ	خ	خ
بَطِّيخ	نَخْلَة	خَرُوف
Batteekh	Nakhla	Kharoof

خ

Trace it: خطط:

خ

خ

خ

ضَعْ دَائِرَةْ حَوْلْ اَلْكَلِمَاتْ اَلتِي تَحْتَوِي عَلَى حَرِفُ اَلْ خ

Circle the words that have the letter Khaa'

مَحْبَز   حَقِيبَة   تَارِيخ

خَشَب

بَاب

أَصْفَر   خَمْسَة

وَرقة   خُوخ   صَخْرَة

LONG AND SHORT VOWELS

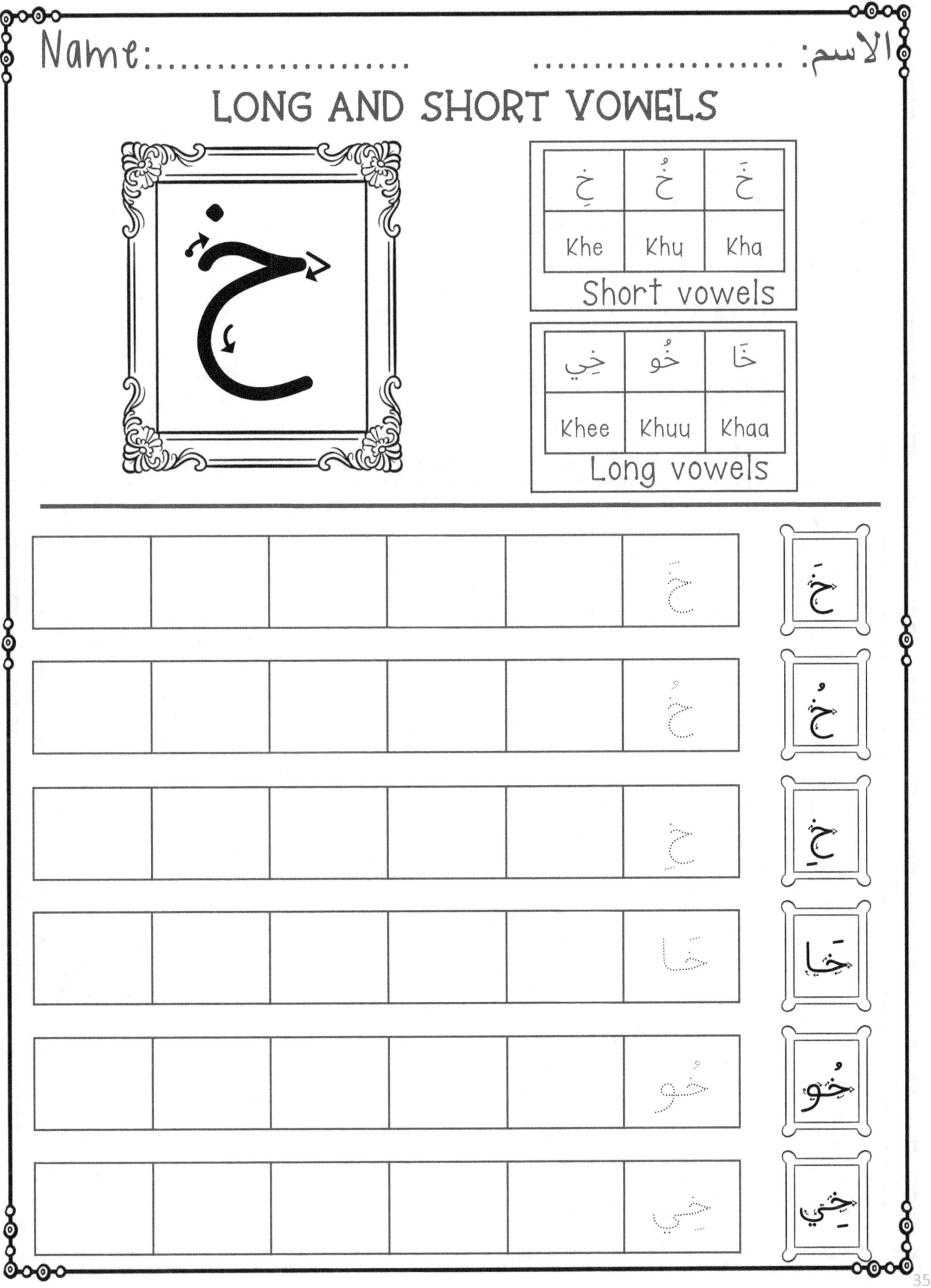

خِ	خُ	خَ
Khe	Khu	Kha

Short vowels

خِي	خُو	خَا
Khee	Khuu	Khaa

Long vowels

Name:...............

حَرْفُ الدَّال

Daal

This letter doesn't connect to the letter after it

لَوِّنْ:

Color:

Dajaaja

دَجَاجَة

Daal

دَال

د

Trace it:

خَطِّطْ:

 دِ

 دِ

 دِ

 دِ

Name:...................... .... :الاسم

This letter doesn't connect to the letter after it

حَرْفُ الدَّال

Daal

At the end	In the middle	In the beginning
ـد	ـد	د
فَهْد	هَدِيَّة	دُب
Fahd	Hadiyya	Dob

Trace it: خَطِّط:

ـد

ـد

د

ضَعْ دَائِرَةْ حَوْلْ ٱلْكَلِمَاتْ ٱلَّتِي تَحْتَوِي عَلَى حَرِفْ ٱلـ د

Circle the words that have the letter Dal

دَلُو   بَنَفْسَجِي   مَدْرَسَة

يَد   ضَوْء

أَسَد   صُنْدُوق

دَفْتَر   قَلَم   قَمَر

37

LONG AND SHORT VOWELS

دِ	دُ	دَ
De	Du	Da

Short vowels

دِي	دُو	دَا
Dee	Duu	Daa

Long vowels

This letter doesn't connect to the letter after it

Name:....................... .... :الاسم

حَرْفُ الذَّال

Thaal

This letter doesn't connect to the letter after it

Color: لَوِّنْ: ذ

Thora   Thaal

ذُِرَة   ذَال

Trace it: خَطِّط:

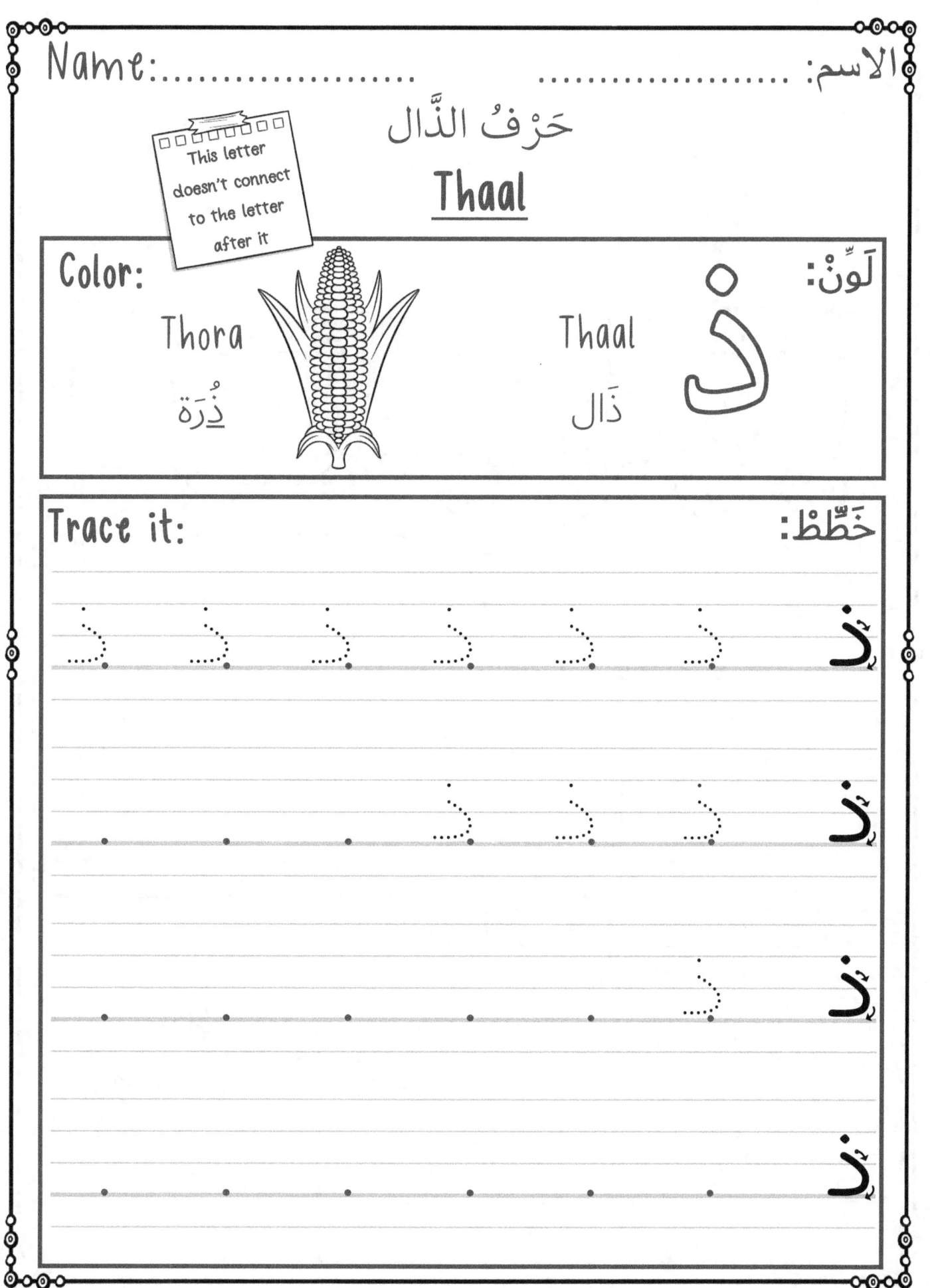

ذ

ذ

ذ

ذ

Name:.........................

This letter doesn't connect to the letter after it

حَرْفُ الذَّال

Thaal

At the end	In the middle	In the beginning
ـذْ	ـذ	ذ
قُنْفُذ	نَافِذَة	ذُبَاب
Qonfoth	Naafitha	Thobaab

ذ ◇

Trace it: خطّظ:

ذ .... • • •

ذ .... • • •

ذ .... • • •

ضَعْ دَائِرَةً حَوْلَ ٱلْكَلِمَاتْ ٱلَّتِي تَحْتَوِي عَلَى حَرِفْ ٱلْ ذ

Circle the words that have the letter Thaal

غِذَاء   بُرْتُقَالِي   ذِئْب

عَصِير   جَبَل

ذَهَب   حِذَاء

أُسْتَاذ   دَرَج   تِلْمِيذ

LONG AND SHORT VOWELS

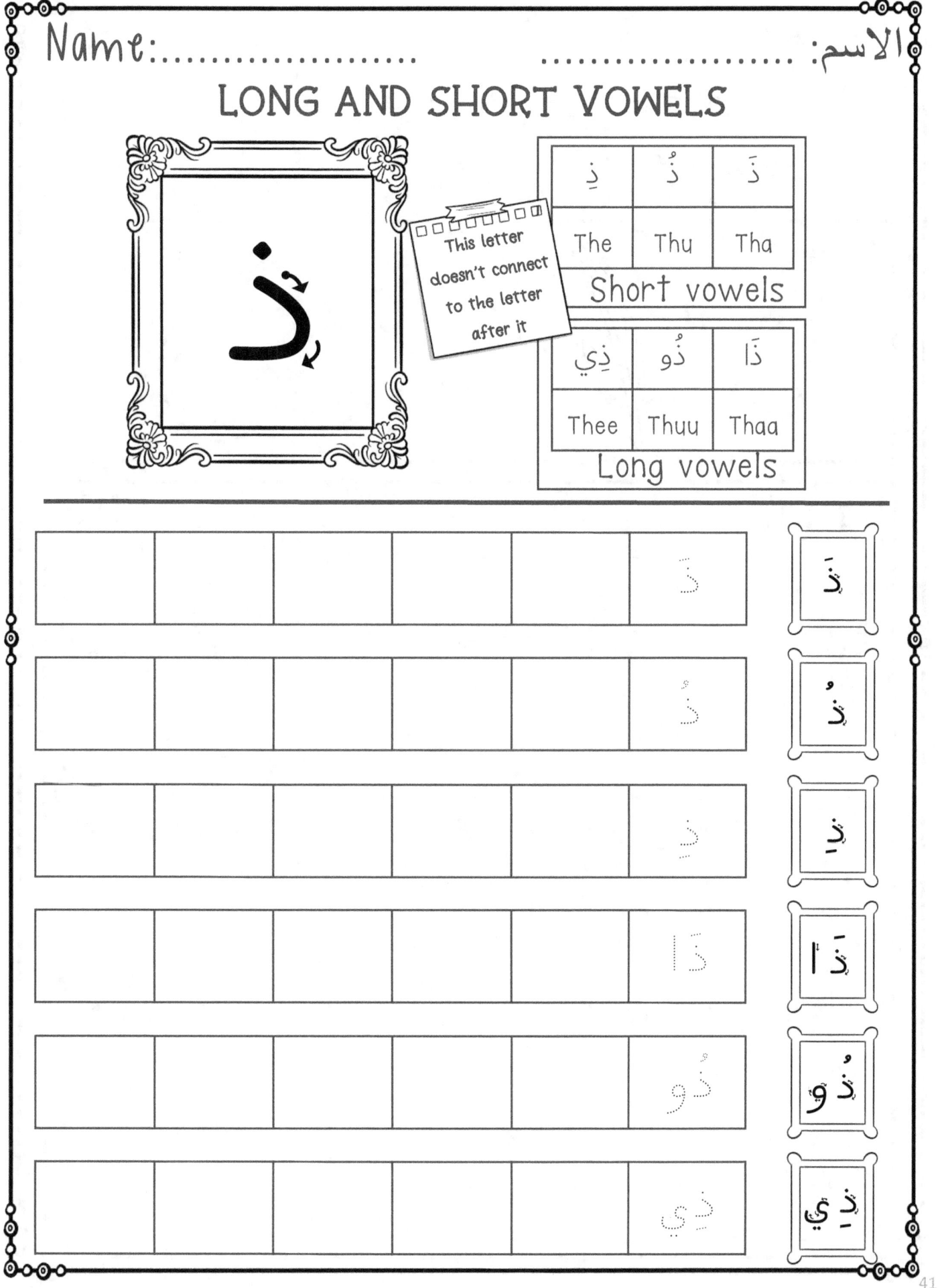

This letter doesn't connect to the letter after it

ذِ	ذُ	ذَ
The	Thu	Tha

Short vowels

ذِي	ذُو	ذَا
Thee	Thuu	Thaa

Long vowels

حَرْفُ الرَّاء
Raa'

This letter doesn't connect to the letter after it

Color: لَوِّنْ:

Reesha

رِيشَة

Raa'

رَاء

ر

Trace it: خَطِّطْ:

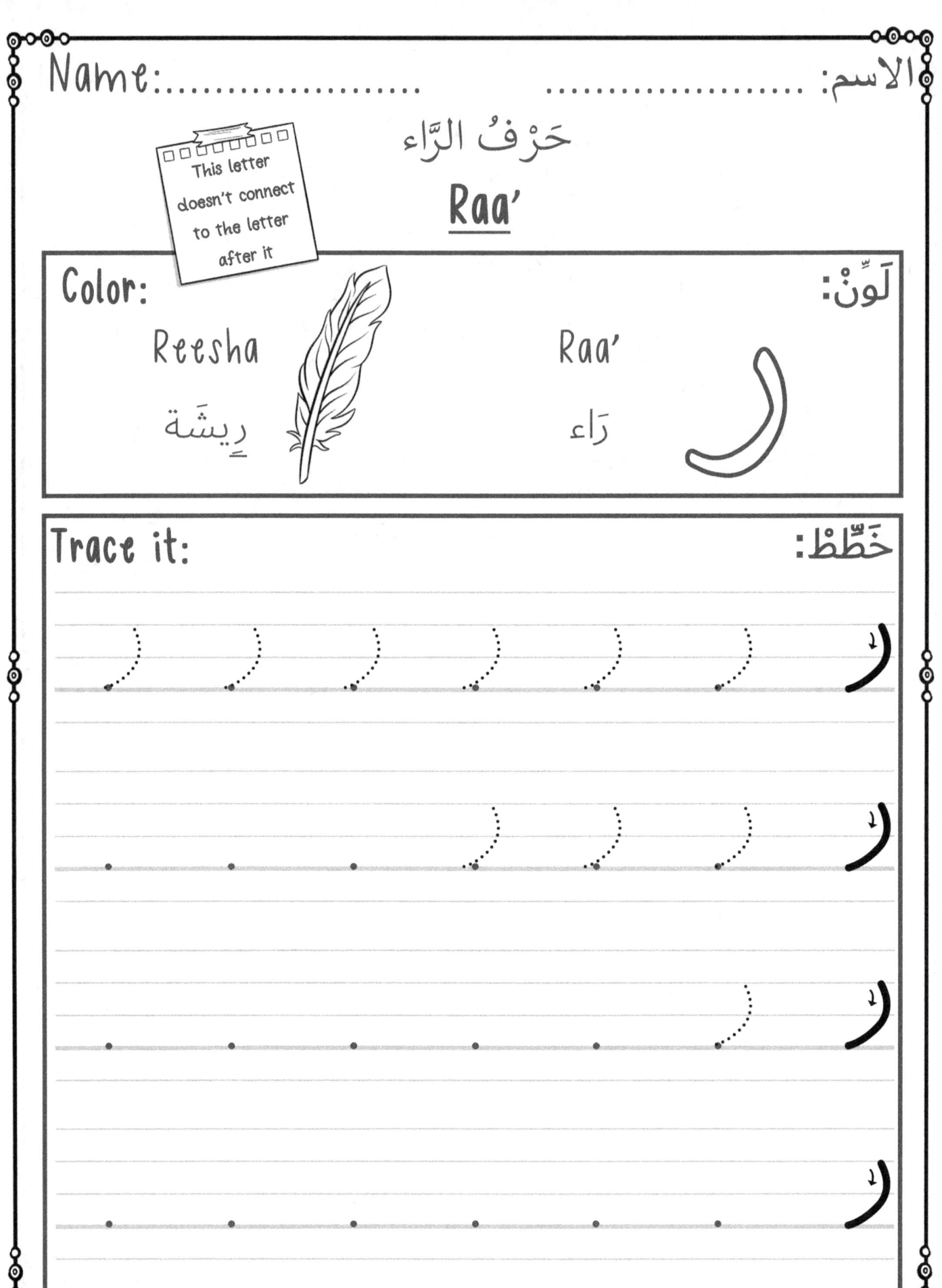

Name:...................... الاسم :................

This letter doesn't connect to the letter after it

حَرْفُ الرَّاء

Raa'

At the end	In the middle	In the beginning
ﺭ	ﺭ	ﺭ
بَحْر	بُرْتُقَال	رَمْل
Bahr	Bortoqaal	Raml

Trace it: خَطِّط :

ر

ر

ر

ضَعْ دَائِرَةً حَوْلَ ٱلْكَلِمَاتْ ٱلَّتِي تَحْتَوِي عَلَى حَرِفِ ٱلْ ر

Circle the words that have the letter Raa'

عُشُب   رَمْل   مَسْبَح

أَرُز   شَعِير

هَاتِف   رُمَّان

عَصِير   حَافِلَة   إِبْرِيق

43

LONG AND SHORT VOWELS

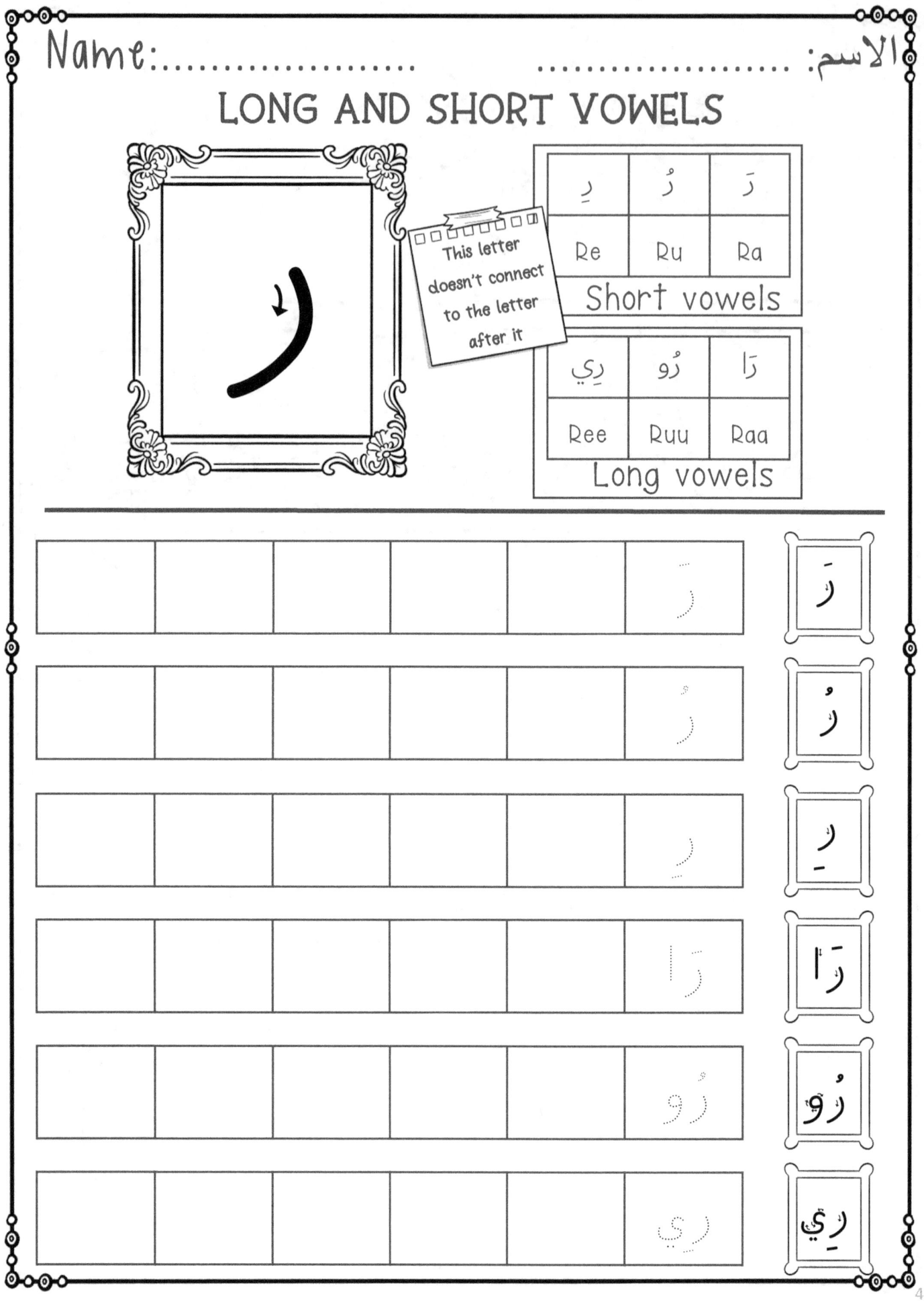

This letter doesn't connect to the letter after it

رِ	رُ	رَ
Re	Ru	Ra

Short vowels

رِي	رُو	رَا
Ree	Ruu	Raa

Long vowels

Name:.................... .... : الاسْم

حَرْفُ الزَّيْن

Zayn

لَوِّنْ:   ز

Color:

Zaraafa   Zayn

زَرَافَة   زَيْن

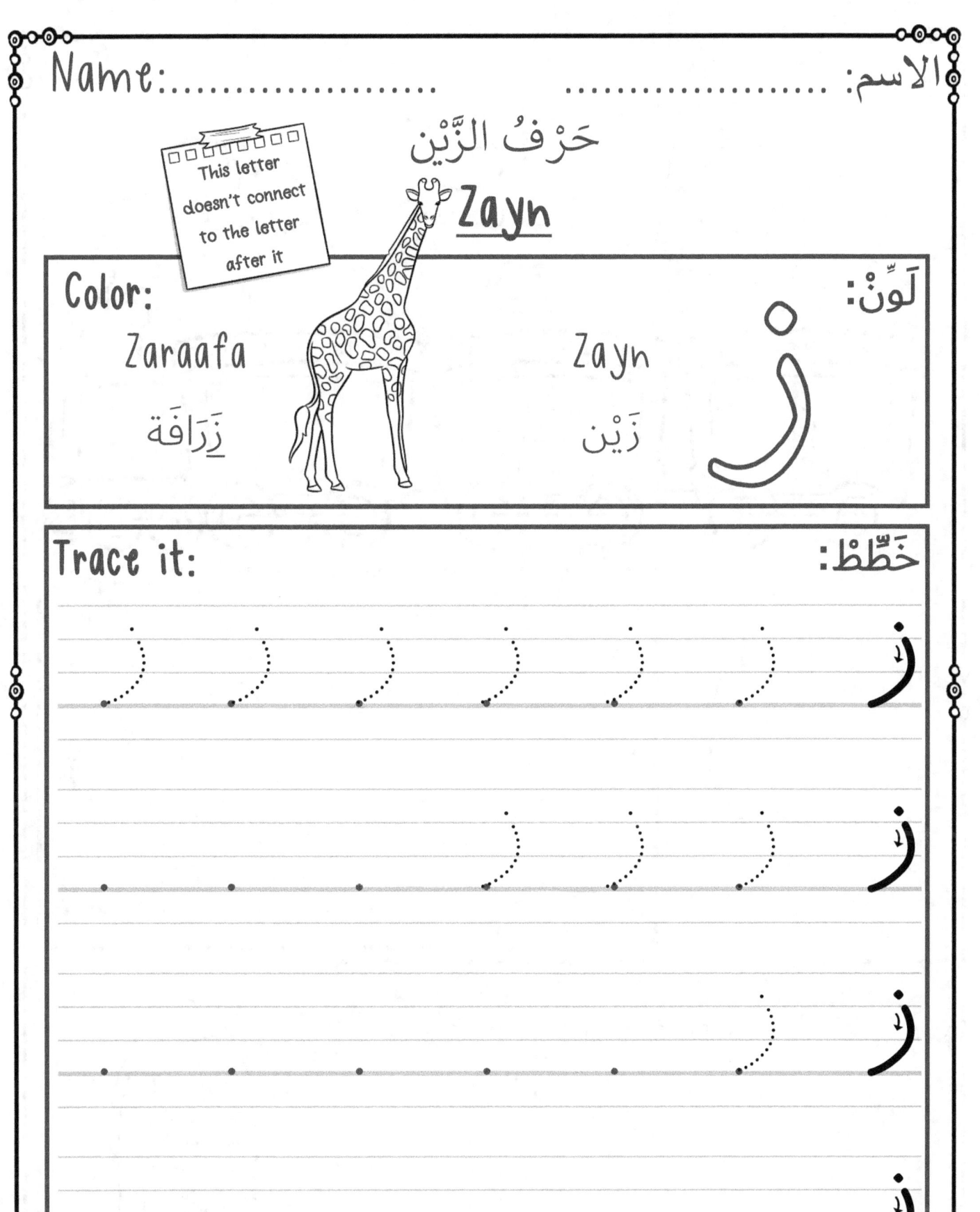

Trace it: خَطِّظ:

ز

ز

ز

ز

This letter doesn't connect to the letter after it

حَرْفُ الزَّيْن

Zayn

At the end	In the middle	In the beginning
ـز	ـزـ	ز
خُبْز	مَنْزِل	زَيْت
Khubz	Manzel	Zayt

ز

Trace it: خَطِّط:

ـز
ـزـ
ـزـ

ضَعْ دَائِرَةً حَوْلَ الْكَلِمَاتْ الَّتِي تَحْتَوِي عَلَى حَرِفْ آلْ ز

Circle the words that have the letter Zayn

أَزْرَق   أَرِز

حَائِط

مِيزَان

بَقَرَة

أَلْوَان   زَرَافَة

زَهْرَة   مَوْز   طِفِل

46

LONG AND SHORT VOWELS

زِ	زُ	زَ
Ze	Zu	Za

Short vowels

زِي	زُو	زَا
Zee	Zuu	Zaa

Long vowels

This letter doesn't connect to the letter after it

حَرْفُ السِّين

Seen

Color:		لَوِّنْ:
Samaka		Seen
سَمَكَة		سِين

س

Trace it: خَطِّطْ:

ﻳِﺲ

ﻳِﺲ

ﻳِﺲ

ﻳِﺲ

Name:.................... 　　　　............. :الاسم

حَرْفُ السِّين

Seen

At the end	In the middle	In the beginning
س	ـسـ	سـ
خَسّ	عَسَل	سَيَّارَة
Khas	Asal	Sayyaara

Trace it: 　　　　　　　　　　　خَطِّط :

بِيد

بِيد

عِين

Circle the words that have the letter Seen

سَمَاء　　　　صَافِي

مَسْبَح

مَسَاء　　شَمِس

دَائِرَة　　حَفْلَة

أَوْلَاد　سِلْسَال　يَابِس

LONG AND SHORT VOWELS

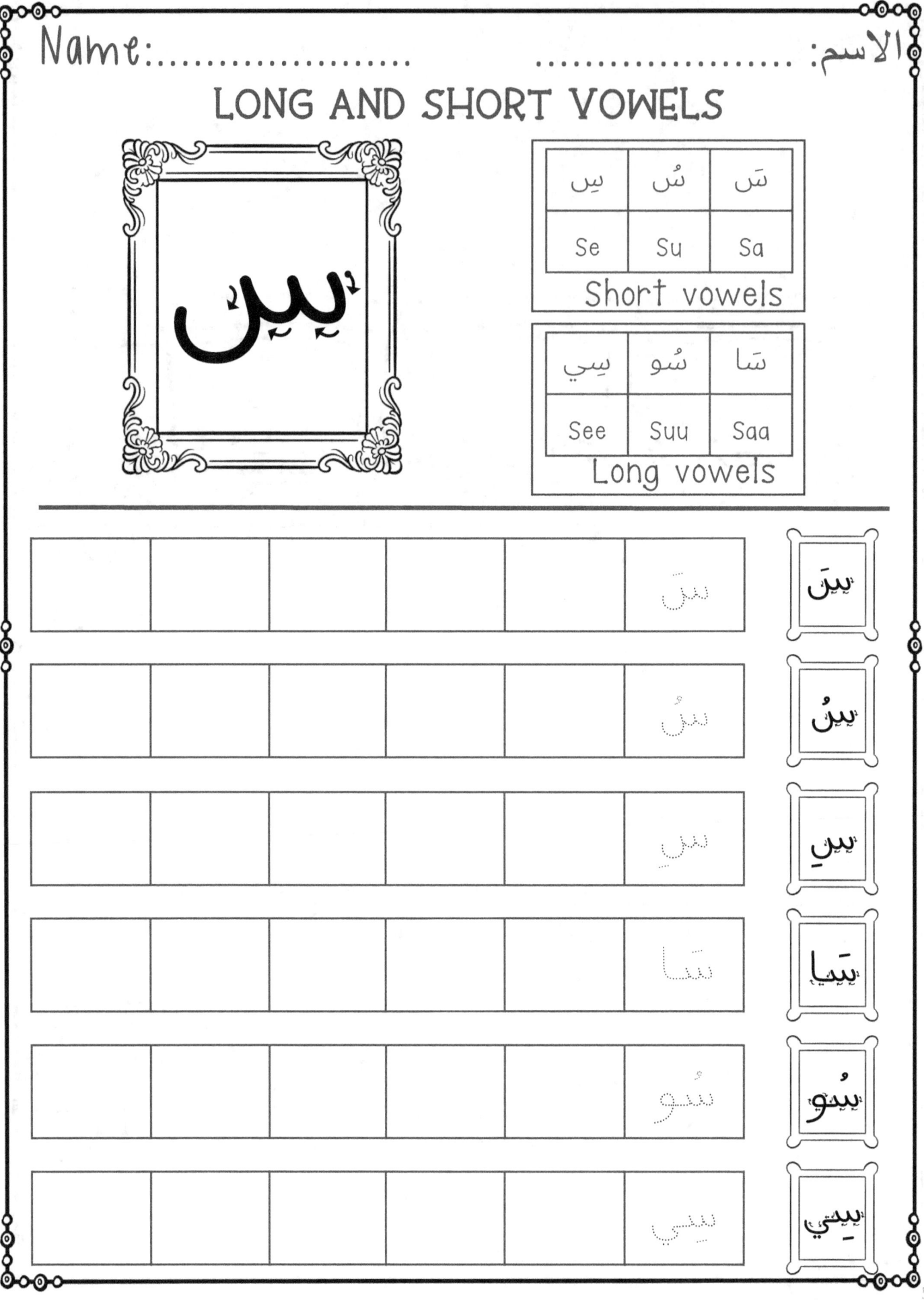

سَ	سُ	سِ
Sa	Su	Se

Short vowels

سَا	سُو	سِي
Saa	Suu	See

Long vowels

حَرْفُ الشِّين

<u>Sheen</u>

لَوِّنْ:		Color:

Shames   Sheen

شَمِس   شِين

ش

Trace it: خَطِّظْ:

شِ   شِ   شِ   شِ   شِ   شِ   شِ

شِ   شِ   شِ   شِ   شِ   شِ

شِ   شِ

شِ

Name:................... الاسم: .... :

حَرْفُ الشِّين

Sheen

At the end	In the middle	In the beginning
ش	شـ	ش
رِيش	مِنْشَا	شَمْس
Rish	Menshaar	Shams

خَطِّظْ : Trace it:

بْش   نْشـ

عْش   نْشـ

عْش   نْشـ

ش

ضَعْ دَائِرَةً حَوْلَ الْكَلِمَاتْ الَّتِي تَحْتَوِي عَلَى حَرِفْ الْ ش
Circle the words that have the letter Sheen

شَعِر   حَرِف   أَرِض

مِشْمُش   سَطِر

فَرَاشَة   حَشَرَة

تِلْفَاز   شَمِس   عُش

52

Name:........................ .... :الاسم

LONG AND SHORT VOWELS

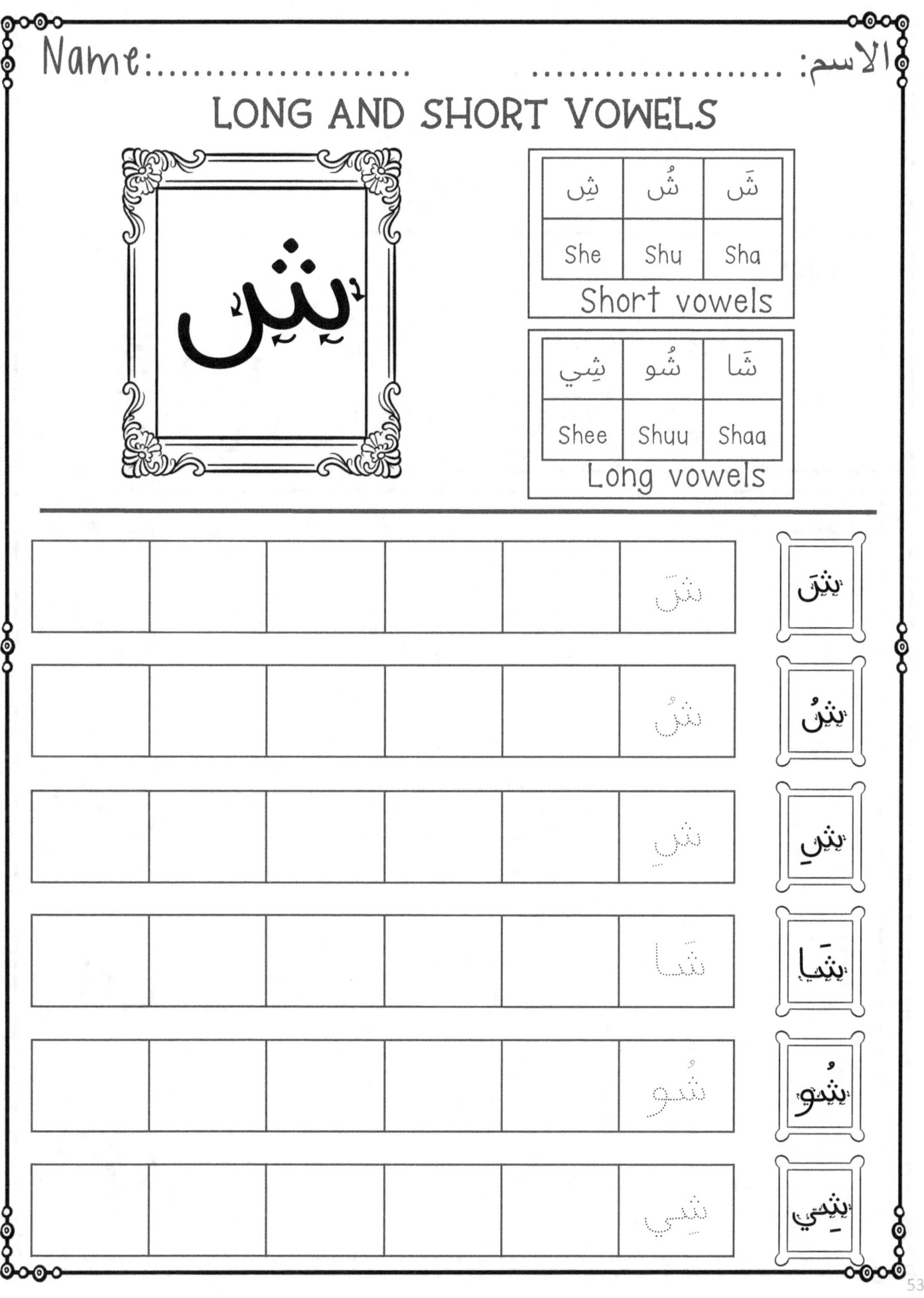

شَ	شُ	شِ
Sha	Shu	She

Short vowels

شَا	شُو	شِي
Shaa	Shuu	Shee

Long vowels

					شَ	شَ
					شُ	شُ
					شِ	شِ
					شَا	شَا
					شُو	شُو
					شِي	شِي

حَرْفُ الصَّاد

Saad

Color: :لَوِّنْ

Soos   Saad

صُوص   صَاد   **ص**

Trace it: :خَطِّط

ص

ص

ص

ص

حَرْفُ الصَّاد

Saad

At the end	In the middle	In the beginning
ص	ـصـ	صـ
قَفَص	بَصَل	صَقر
Qafas	Basal	Saqer

Trace it: خَطِّط:

ص

ص

ص

ضَعْ دَائِرَةً حَوْلَ ٱلْكَلِمَاتْ ٱلِتِي تَحْتَوِي عَلَى حَرْفِ آلْ ص
Circle the words that have the letter Saad

قُصور   صُنْدُوق   بَيْت

سَاعَة   نَبَات

صَحْرَاء   إِجَّاص

مِقَص   حَائِط   فُصُول

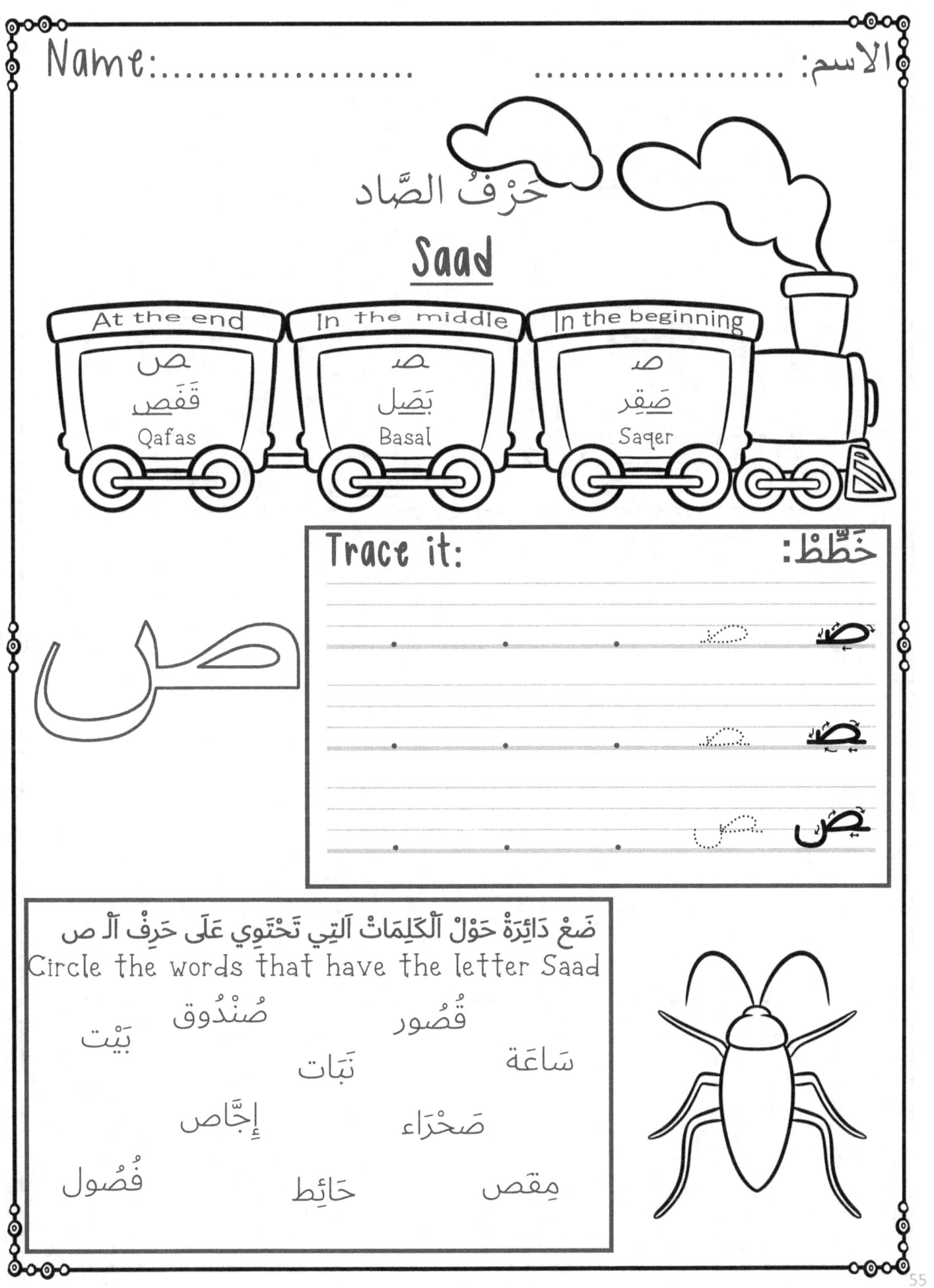

Name:...................

LONG AND SHORT VOWELS

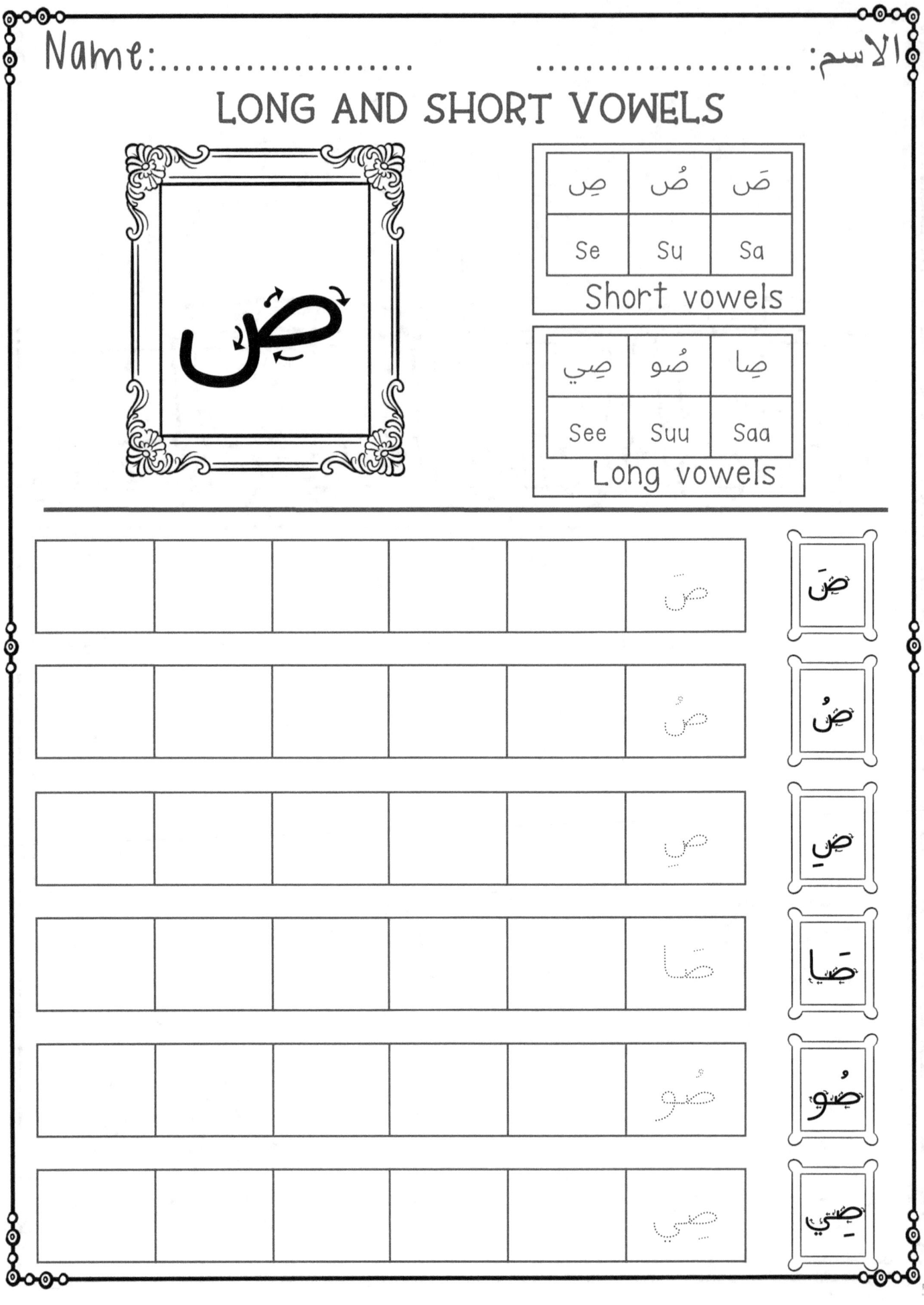

صَ	صُ	صِ
Sa	Su	Se

Short vowels

صَا	صُو	صِي
Saa	Suu	See

Long vowels

حَرْفُ الضَّاد

Dhaad

Color: | لَوِّنْ:

Dafdaa'

Dhaad

ضَاد

ضَفْدَع

ض

Trace it: | خَطِّطْ:

ض

ض

ض

ض

حَرْفُ ٱلْضَّاد

Dhaad

At the end	In the middle	In the beginning
ض	ـضـ	ض
بَيْض	أَخْضَر	ضُيُوف
Bayd	Akhdar	Doyoof

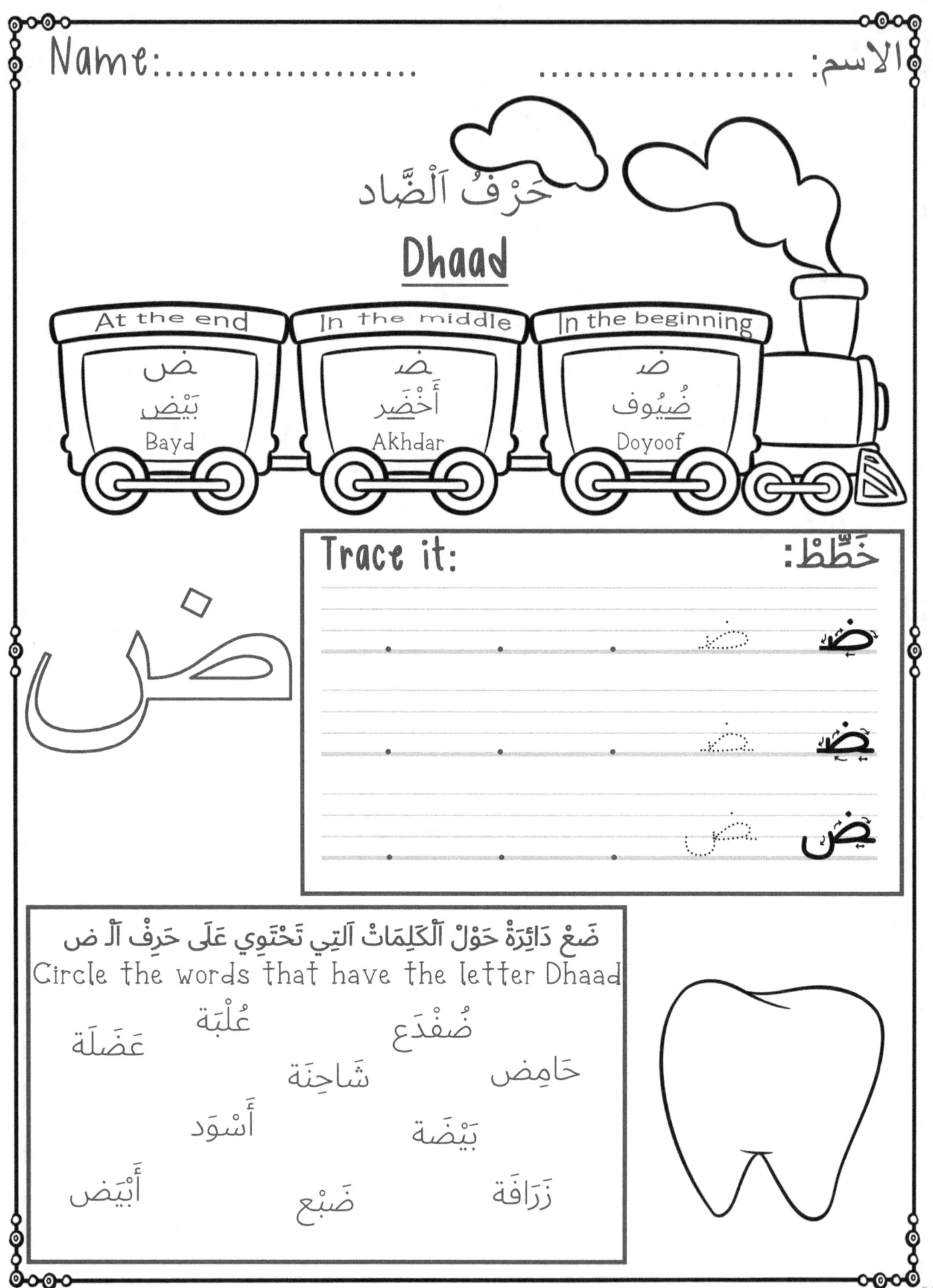

ض

Trace it: خَطِّط:

ضـ

ـضـ

ـض

ضَعْ دَائِرَةً حَوْلَ ٱلْكَلِمَاتْ ٱلتِي تَحْتَوِي عَلَى حَرْفِ ٱلْ ض

Circle the words that have the letter Dhaad

عَضَلَة   عُلْبَة   ضُفْدَع

حَامِض   شَاحِنَة

أَسْوَد   بَيْضَة

أَبْيَض   ضَبْع   زَرَافَة

58

LONG AND SHORT VOWELS

ضِ	ضُ	ضَ
Dhe	Dhu	Dha

Short vowels

ضِي	ضُو	ضَا
Dhee	Dhuu	Dhaa

Long vowels

حَرْفُ ٱلطَّاء

Taa'

Color: لَوِّنْ:

Tareeq

Taa'

طَرِيق

طَاء

Trace it: خَطِّطْ:

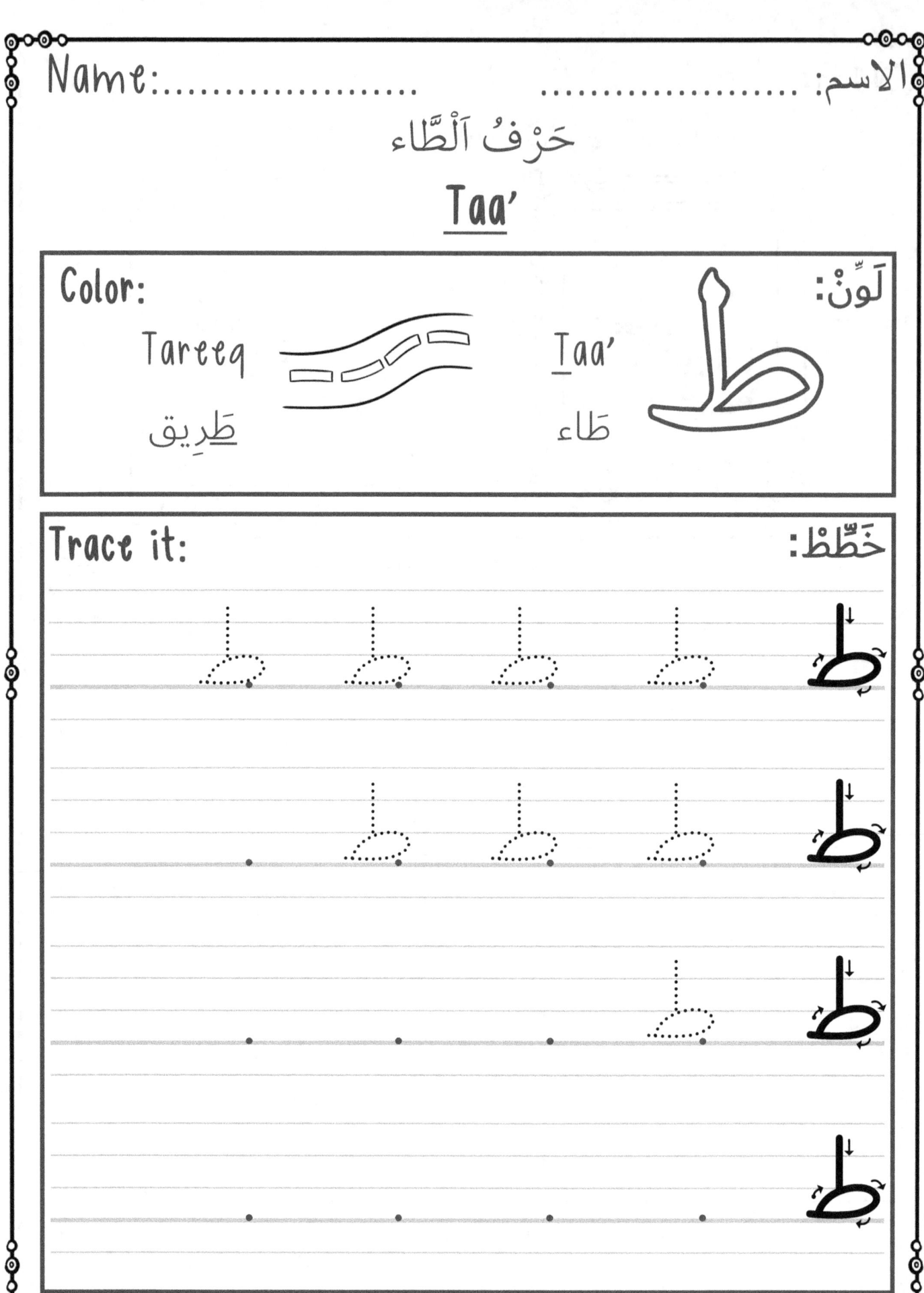

حَرْفُ ٱلطَّاء

Taa'

At the end	In the middle	In the beginning
ط	ط	ط
خَط	بَطْرِيق	طَائِر
khat	Batreeq	Taa'r

Trace it: خَطِّظْ:

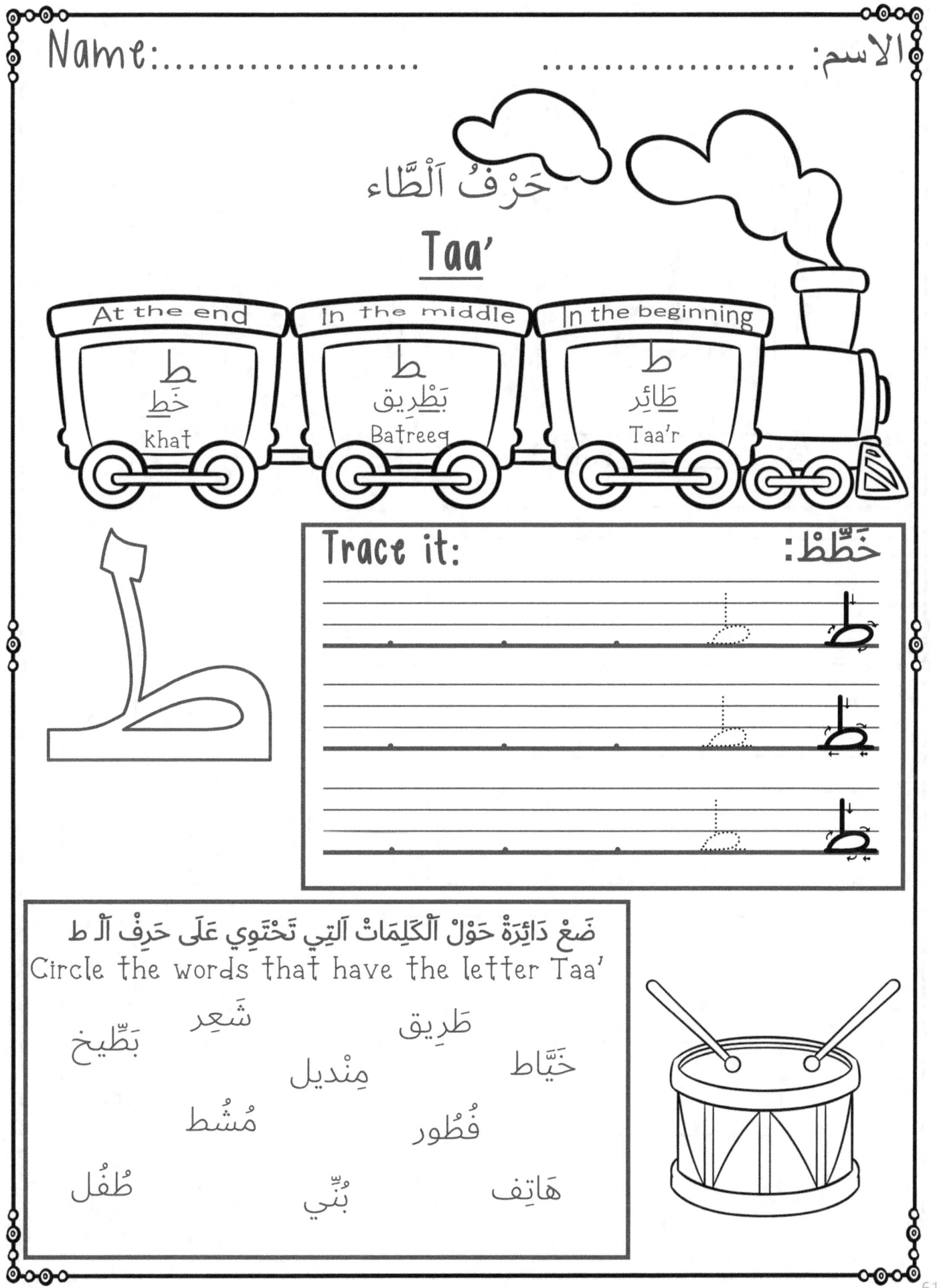

ضَعْ دَائِرَةً حَوْلَ ٱلْكَلِمَاتْ ٱلِتِي تَحْتَوِي عَلَى حَرِفْ ٱلْ ط
Circle the words that have the letter Taa'

طَرِيق   شَعِر   بَطِّيخ

خَيَّاط   مِنْديل

فُطُور   مُشُط

هَاتِف   بُنِّي   طُفُل

LONG AND SHORT VOWELS

طِ	طُ	طَ
Te	Tu	Ta

Short vowels

طِي	طُو	طَا
Tee	Tuu	Taa

Long vowels

حَرْفُ ٱلظَّاء

Zaa'

Color: لَوِّنْ:

Zarf

ظَرْف

Zaa'

ظَاء

ظ

Trace it: خطّظ:

ظ

ظ

ظ

ظ

حَرْفُ اَلْظَّاء

Zaa'

At the end	In the middle	In the beginning
ظ	ظ	ظ
حَظْ	نَظَّارَة	ظَلَام
Haz	Nazaara	Zalaam

ظ

Trace it: خَطِّط :

ظ

ظ

ظ

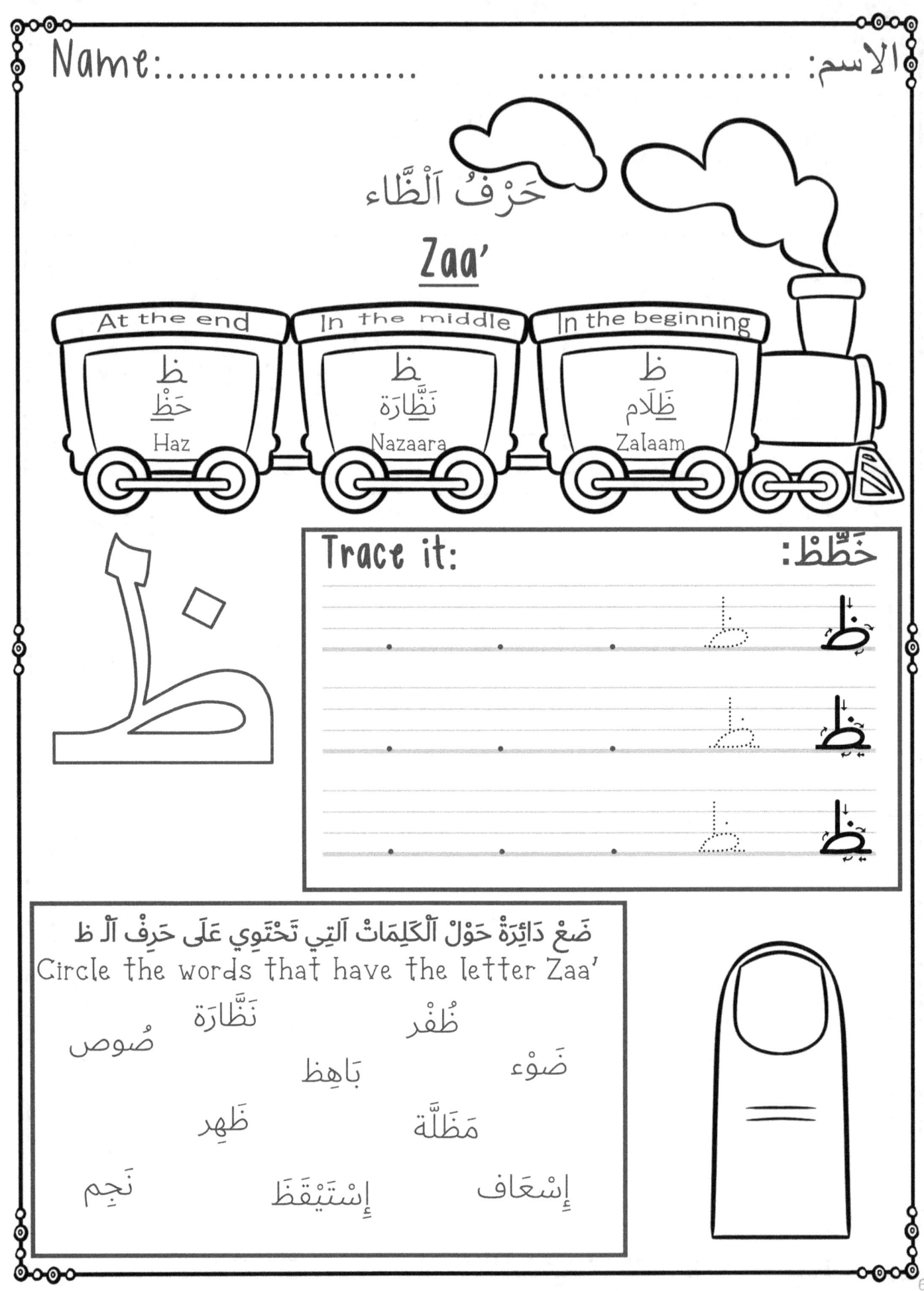

ضَعْ دَائِرَة حَوْلَ اَلْكَلِمَاتُ اَلتِي تَحْتَوِي عَلَى حَرْفُ اَلْ ظ

Circle the words that have the letter Zaa'

نَظَّارَة   ظُفُر

صُوص   بَاهِظ   ضَوْء

ظِهِر   مَظَلَّة

نَجم   إِسْتَيْقَظ   إِسْعَاف

LONG AND SHORT VOWELS

ظِ	ظُ	ظَ
Ze	Zu	Za

Short vowels

ظِي	ظُو	ظَا
Zee	Zuu	Zaa

Long vowels

حَرْفُ اَلْعَيْن

‘**Ain**

Color:		لَوِّنْ: ع

‘Inab
عِنَب

‘Ain
عَيْن

Trace it: خَطِّطْ:

ع

ع

ع

ع

حَرْفُ ٱلْعَيْن

'Ain

At the end	In the middle	In the beginning
ـع	ـعـ	عـ
مَصْنَع	مِلْعَقَة	عَصِير
Masnaa'	Mel'aqa	'Aseer

Trace it: خَطِّطْ:

عـ

ـعـ

ـع

ع

ضَعْ دَائِرَة حَوْلَ ٱلْكَلِمَاتْ ٱلَتِي تَحْتَوِي عَلَى حَرْفِ ٱلْـ ع

Circle the words that have the letter 'Ain

وَرَقَة	عِطْر
رَضِيع	
وَرْدَةْ	مَدْرَسَة
عُش	وَاسِع
إِسْعَاف	خَشَب	سَعِيد

LONG AND SHORT VOWELS

إِ	إُ	إَ
'Ae	'Au	'A

Short vowels

عِي	عُو	عَا
'Aee	'Auu	'Aa

Long vowels

حَرْفُ الغَيْن

Ghain

Color:	لَوِّنْ:

Ghayma   Ghain   غ

غَيْمة   غَيْن

Trace it:	خَطِّطْ:

غ   غ   غ   غ   غ   غ

غ   غ   غ   غ

غ   غ

غ

حَرْفُ الغَيْن

Ghain

At the end	In the middle	In the beginning
غ	غ	غ
صُمُغ	بَبَغَاء	غَزَال
Somogh	Babaghaa'	Ghazaal

Trace it: خَطِّط:

غ

غ

غ

ضَعْ دَائِرَة حَوْل الْكَلِمَاتْ الَتِي تَحْتَوِي عَلَى حَرِف الْـ غ
Circle the words that have the letter Ghain

نَظَّارَة   مَضْغ

وَرْدِي

مَغْسَلة   غَزَال

مَبْلَغ   جَمَل

غُرَاب   رَغْوَة   خِيَار

LONG AND SHORT VOWELS

غِ	غُ	غَ
Ghe	Ghu	Gha

Short vowels

غِي	غُو	غَا
Ghee	Ghuu	Ghaa

Long vowels

حَرْفُ الفَاء

Faa'

لَوِّنْ: Color:	ف

Faraashah   Faa' فَاء

فِرَاشَة

خَطِّطْ: Trace it:

ف

ف

ف

ف

Name:.......................

حَرْفُ الفَاء

Faa'

At the end	In the middle	In the beginning
ـف	ـفـ	ف
هَاتِف	طُفُل	فِيل
Haatef	Tofol	Feel

Trace it:

خَطِّط :

ف

ـفـ

ـف

ضَعْ دَائِرَةْ حَوْلْ ٱلْكَلِمَاتْ ٱلِّتي تَحْتَوِي عَلَى حَرْف ٱلْ ف

Circle the words that have the letter Faa'

دَفْتَر   تَاج

نَهِر

فَم   طَاوِلَة

فَأْرَة   خَرُوف

قِفْل

مِعْطَف   حَلِيب

LONG AND SHORT VOWELS

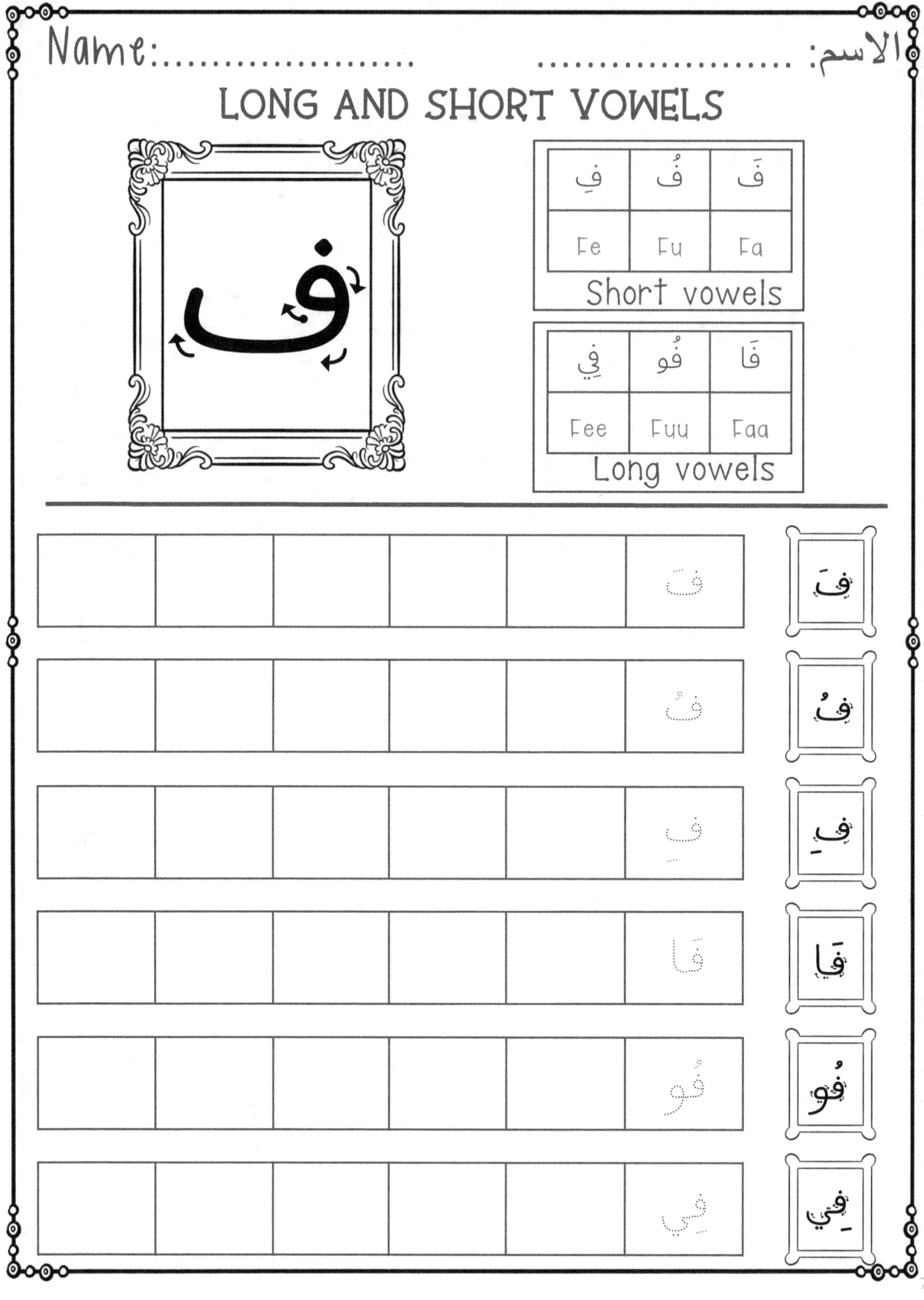

فَ	فُ	فِ
Fe	Fu	Fa

Short vowels

فَ	فُو	فِي
Fee	Fuu	Faa

Long vowels

حَرْفُ القَاف

Qaaf

Color: | لَوِّنْ:

Qamar

قَمَر

Qaaf

قَاف

ق

Trace it: | خُطِّطْ:

ق

ق

ق

ق

حَرْفُ القَاف

Qaaf

At the end	In the middle	In the beginning
ق	ـقـ	ق
صَدِيق	فَقَرَة	قَلِب
Sadeeq	Faqara	Qaleb

Trace it: خَطِّط :

ق

قِ

ق

ضَعْ دَائِرَة حَوْلَ الْكَلِمَاتُ الَّتِي تَحْتَوِي عَلَى حَرِفْ آلْ ق

Circle the words that have the letter Qaaf

كَلْب   هُدْهُد

بَقَرَة   قَلَم

صَقْر

رَأْس   حَبَق

قُبَّعَة   أَرْنَب   صُنْدُوق

Name:.................... .... الاسم:

LONG AND SHORT VOWELS

قَ	قُ	قِ
Qa	Qu	Qee

Short vowels

قَا	قُو	قِي
Qaa	Quu	Qee

Long vowels

Name:...................

حَرْفُ الكَاف

Kaaf

لَوِّنْ:

ك

Color:

Ketaab

كِتَاب

Kaaf

كَاف

خَطِّطْ:

Trace it:

حَرْفُ الكَاف

Kaaf

At the end	In the middle	In the beginning
ك	ـكـ	ك
سَمَك	مَكْتَب	كُتُب
Samak	Maktab	Kotob

Trace it: خَطِّطْ:

ك

ـكـ

ـكـ

ضَعْ دَائِرَةً حَوْلَ الْكَلِمَاتْ الَّتِي تَحْتَوِي عَلَى حَرِفْ آلْ ك
Circle the words that have the letter Kaaf

كَعْكَة   دِيك

مَلِك

أَحْمَر   كَلِمَة

كَرَز   عَنْكَبُوت

غَابَة   بَطْرِيق   فَحِم

LONG AND SHORT VOWELS

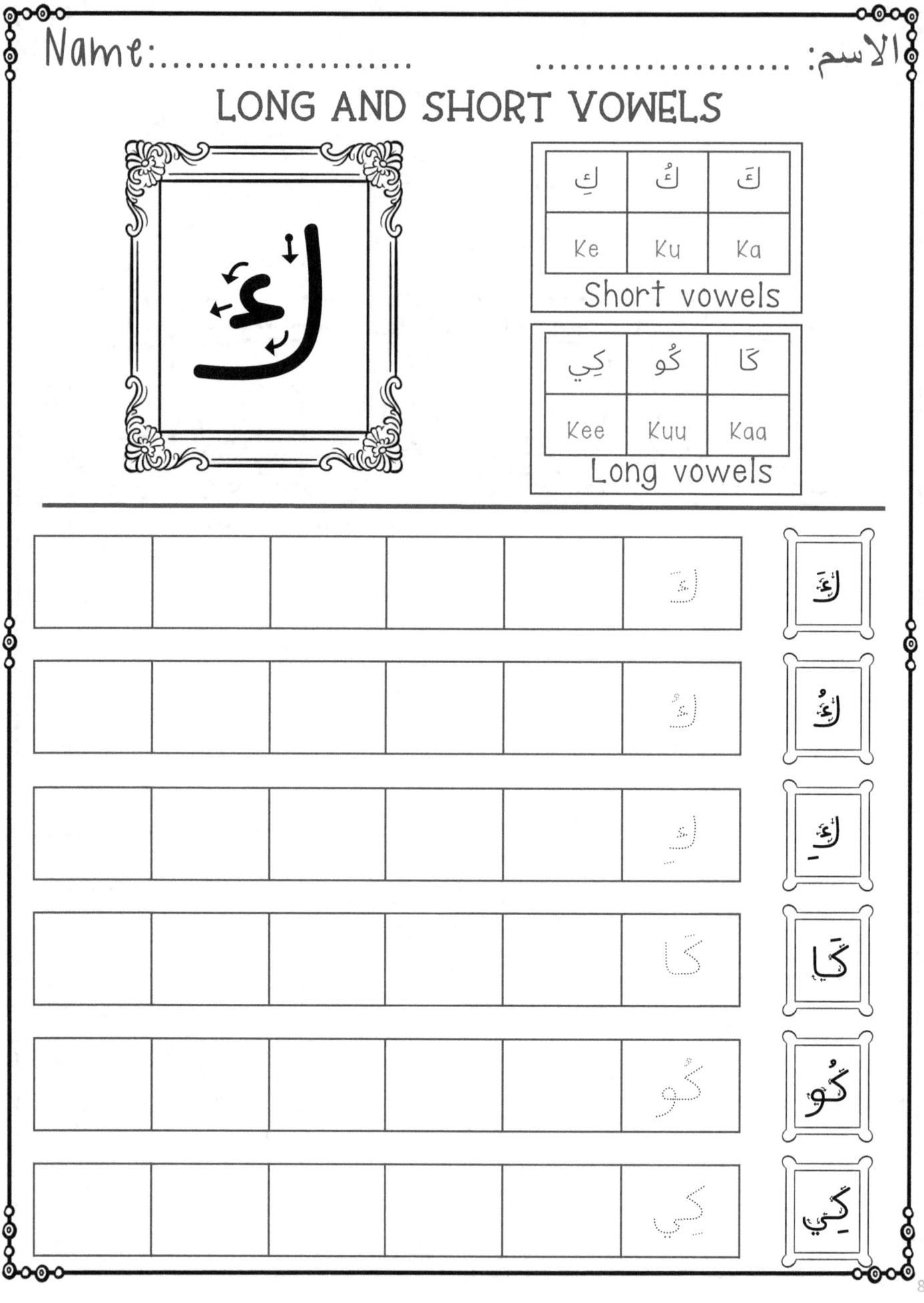

كِ	كُ	كَ
Ke	Ku	Ka

Short vowels

كِي	كُو	كَا
Kee	Kuu	Kaa

Long vowels

حَرْفُ اللَّام

Laam

Color: لَوِّنْ:

Lawz لَوْز

Laam لَام

ل

Trace it: خَطِّطْ:

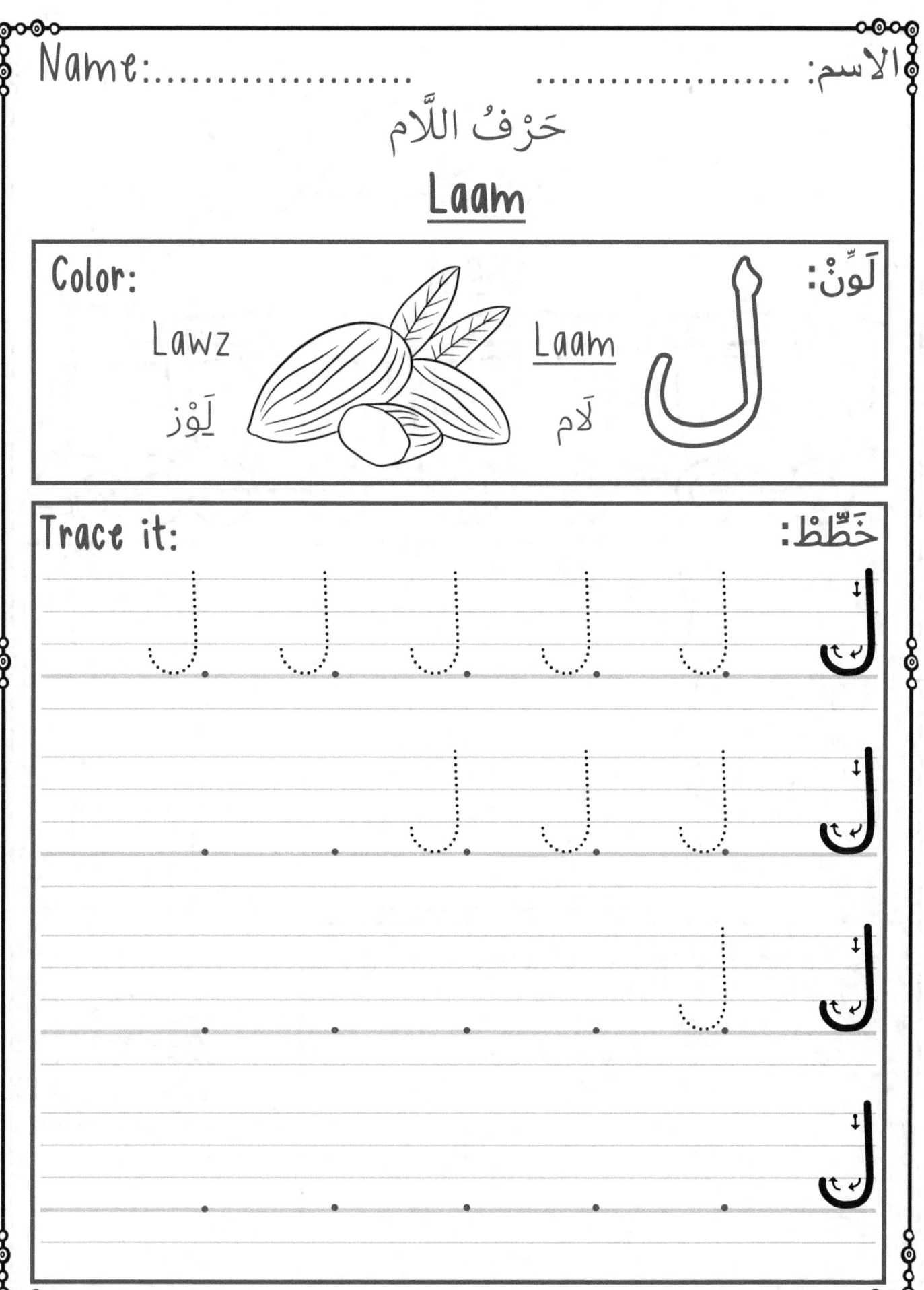

حَرْفُ اللَّام

Laam

At the end	In the middle	In the beginning
ل	ـلـ	لـ
بِصلْ	تِلْفَازْ	لَبَنْ
Basal	Telfaaz	Laban

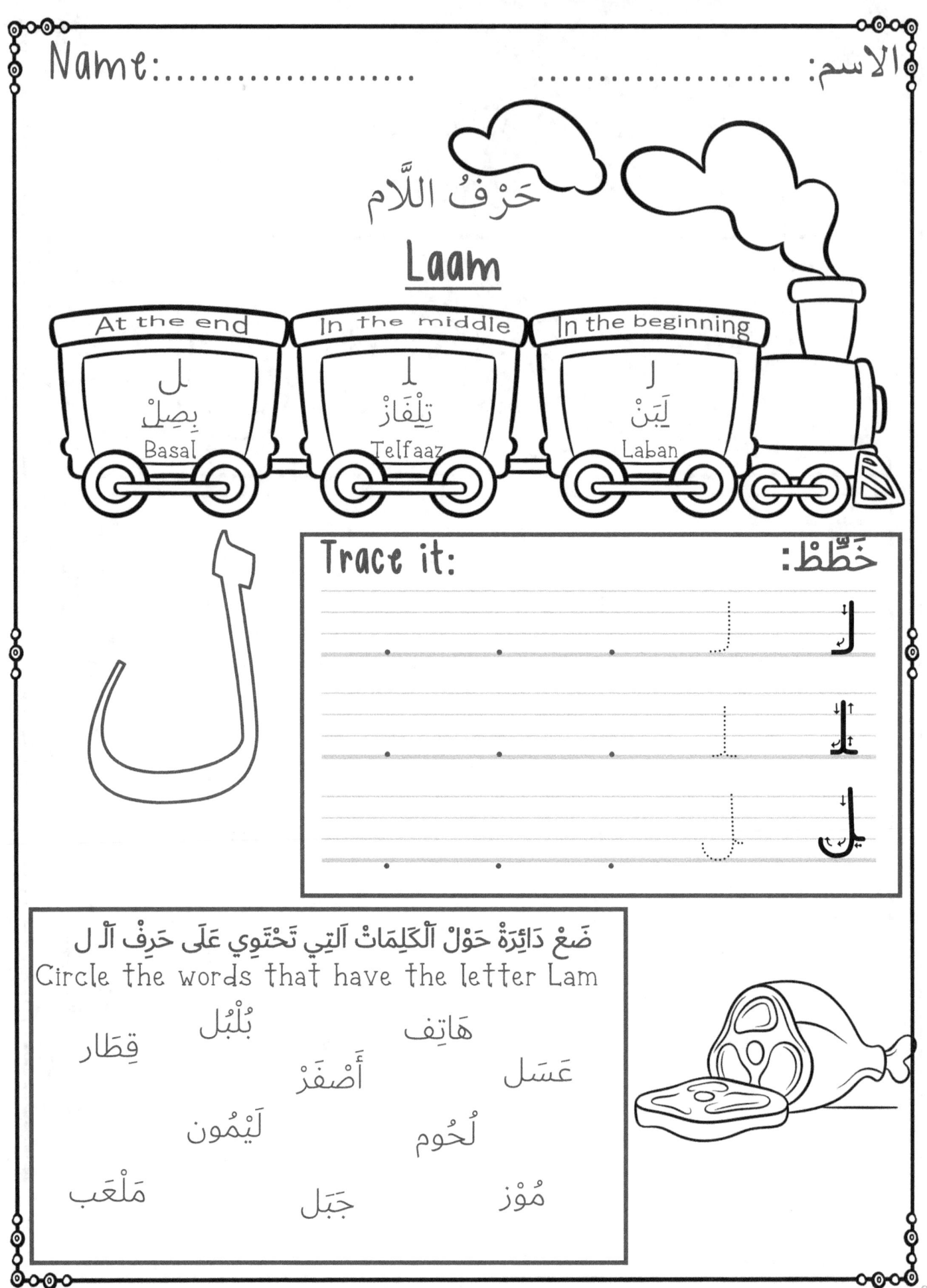

Trace it: خَطِّطْ:

أ

ـلـ

لـ

ضَعْ دَائِرَةً حَوْلَ الْكَلِمَاتْ الَّتِي تَحْتَوِي عَلَى حَرِفْ الـْ ل

Circle the words that have the letter Lam

قِطَار	بُلْبُل	هَاتِف
	أَصْفَر	عَسَل
لَيْمُون	لُحُوم	
مَلْعَب	جَبَل	مُوْز

LONG AND SHORT VOWELS

لِ	لُ	لَ
Le	Lu	La

Short vowels

لِي	لُو	لَا
Lee	Luu	Laa

Long vowels

حَرْفُ المِيم

Meem

| Color: | | لوِّن: |

Mawza

Meem

مَوْزَة

مَيم

Trace it: خَطّط:

مَ

مَ

مَ

مَ

حَرْفُ المِيم

Meem

At the end	In the middle	In the beginning
مـ	ـمـ	مـ
قَلَم	نَمِل	مَوْز
Qalam	Namel	Mawz

Trace it: خَطِّط:

مـ

ـمـ

ـم

م

ضَعْ دَائِرَةْ حَوْلْ الْكَلِمَاتْ الّتِي تَحْتَوِي عَلَى حَرِفْ الـ م
Circle the words that have the letter Meem

دُخَّان   مِشْط   شَمْس

عَظِيم   سَاعَة

سَمَك   فَقَرَة

أَسْوَد   هَرَم   مِقَص

LONG AND SHORT VOWELS

مِ	مُ	مَ
Me	Mu	Ma

Short vowels

مِي	مُو	مَا
Mee	Muu	Maa

Long vowels

حَرْفُ النُّون

Noon

| Color: | | لَوِّنْ: |

Nahlah

نَحْلَة

Noon

نُون

ن

Trace it: خَطِّطْ:

ن

ن

ن

ن

حَرْفُ النُّون

Noon

At the end	In the middle	In the beginning
ـن	ـنـ	نـ
عَيْن	مَنْزِل	نَحْلَة
'Ain	Manzel	Nahla

Trace it: خَطِّطْ:

ن

نـ

ـنـ

ـن

ضَعْ دَائِرَةً حَوْلَ ٱلْكَلِمَاتُ ٱلَتِي تَحْتَوِي عَلَى حَرِفُ آلـ ن

Circle the words that have the letter Noon

قَمْح   نَمْل

مِغْنَاطِيس

سَهْم   مِيزَان

نَيْزَك   سِنْجَاب

خَيْمَة   مِلْعَقَة   سِكِّين

LONG AND SHORT VOWELS

نِ	نُ	نَ
Ne	Nu	Na

Short vowels

نِي	نُو	نَا
Nee	Nuu	Naa

Long vowels

حَرْفُ الهَاء

<u>Ha'</u>

لَوِّنْ:   Color:

Haram   <u>Ha'</u>

هَرَم   هَاء

خَطِّطْ:   Trace it:

حَرْفُ الهَاء

Ha'

At the end	In the middle	In the beginning
ـه	ـهـ	هـ
مِيَاه	فَهْد	هَاتِف
Meeyaah	Fahed	Haatef

Trace it: خَطِّطْ:

هـ

ـهـ

ـه

هـ

ضَعْ دَائِرَةً حَوْلْ الْكَلِمَاتْ الَّتِي تَحْتَوِي عَلَى حَرِفْ آلـ ه
Circle the words that have the letter Haa'

هِرَّة   وَجْه

غِطَاء

دَقِيقَة   إِجَّاص

قِرْدْ   فَاكِهَة

مُنَبِّه   شَهِر   هَوَاء

LONG AND SHORT VOWELS

هـِ	هُـ	هَـ
He	Hu	Ha

Short vowels

هِي	هُو	هَا
Hee	Huu	Haa

Long vowels

Name:................. .... الاسم:

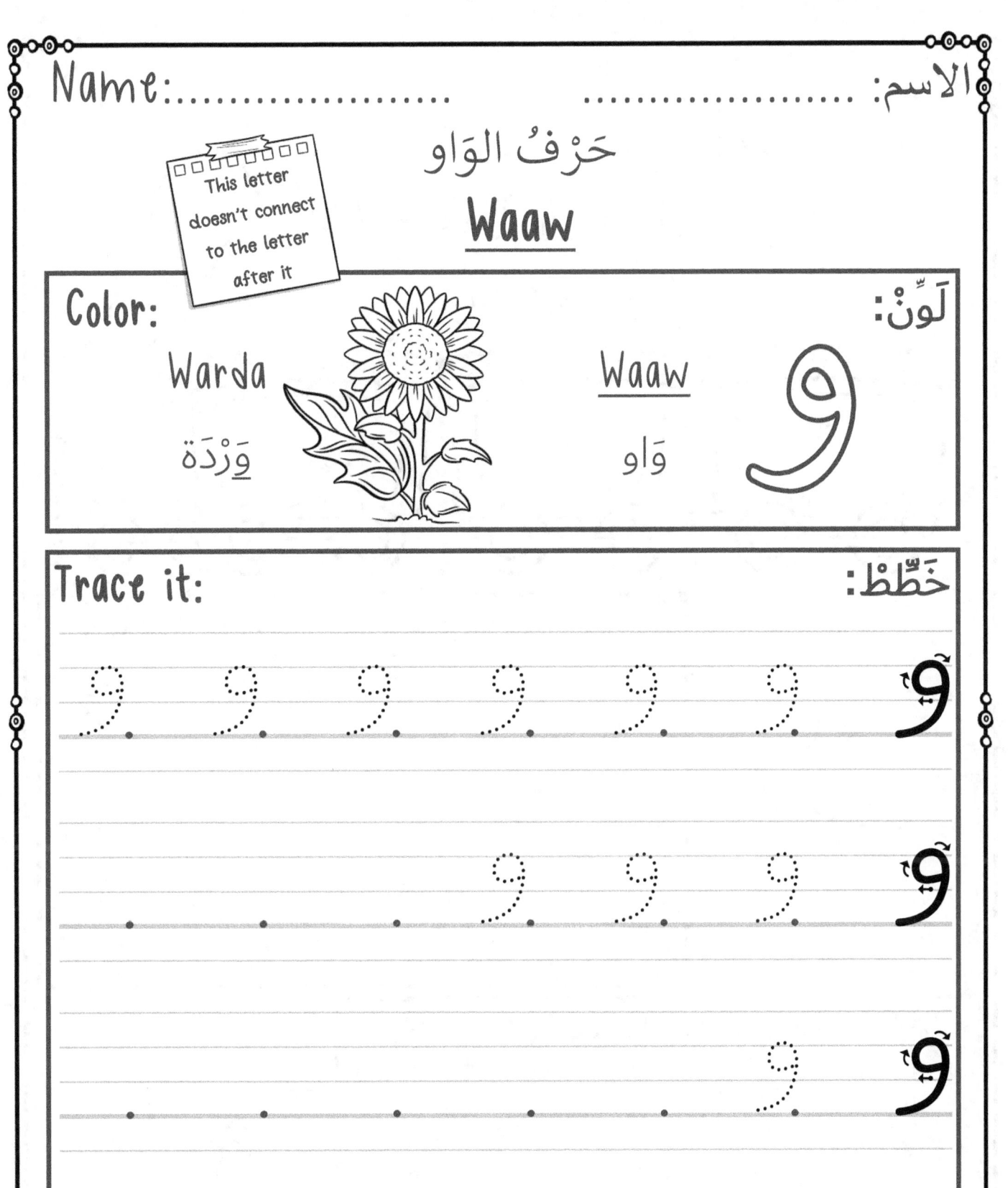

This letter doesn't connect to the letter after it

حَرْفُ الوَاو
Waaw

Color: لَوِّنْ:

Warda

وَرْدَة

Waaw

وَاو

و

Trace it: خَطِّطْ:

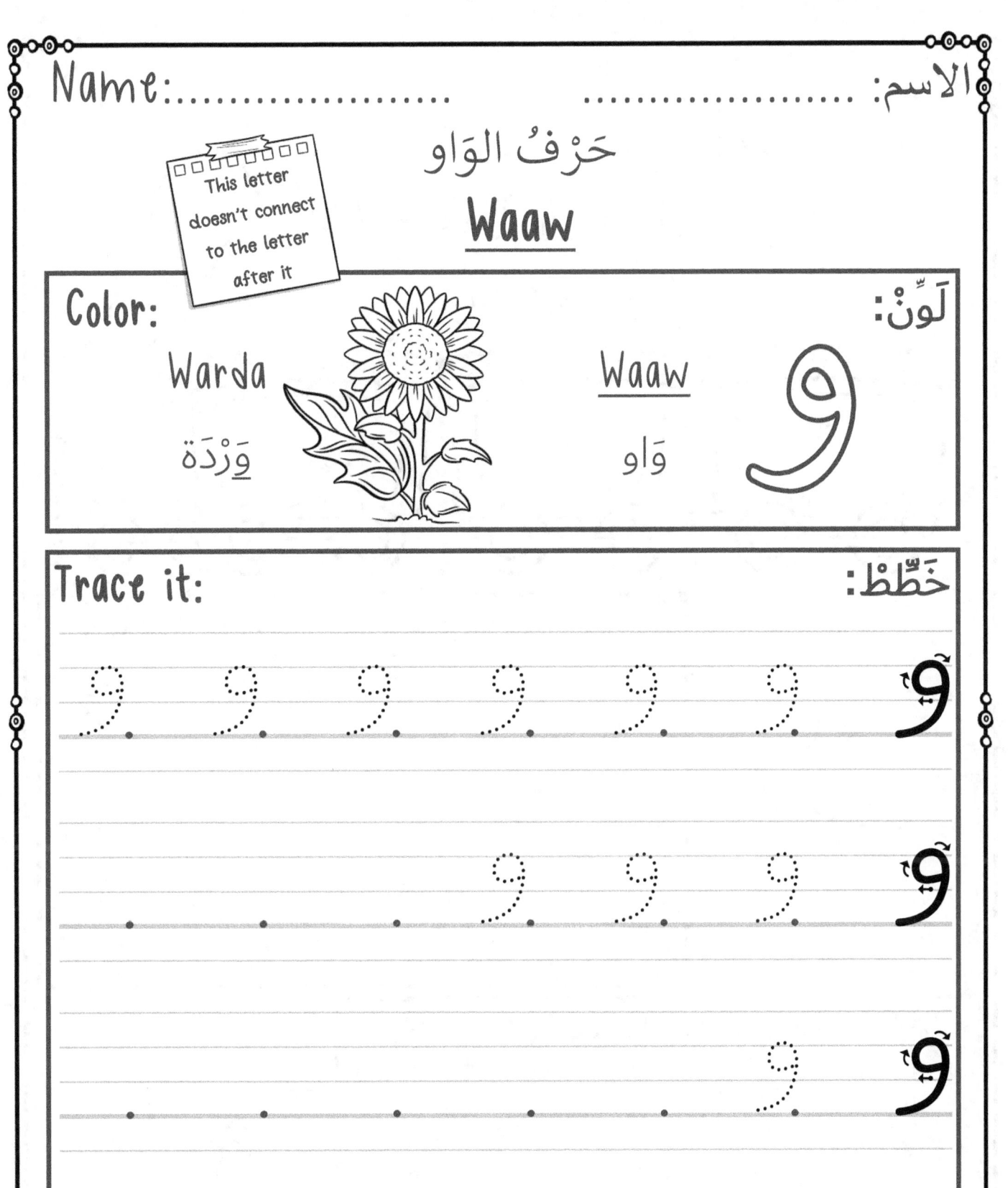

Name:.................

الاسم: ....

This letter doesn't connect to the letter after it

حَرْفُ الْوَاو

Waaw

At the end	In the middle	In the beginning
و	و	و
جَرُو	زَوْرَق	وَرْدَة
Jaroo	Zawrak	Warda

Trace it:

خَطِّط:

و
و
و

و

ضَعْ دَائِرَة حَوْلَ الْكَلِمَاتْ الَتِي تَحْتَوِي عَلَى حَرِفْ الْ و
Circle the words that have the letter Waaw

لَهُو   عُشُب   وِسَادَة

أَرْنَب   هَوَاء

مَطَر   كُرَة

طَاووس   وَجْه   دَلُو

LONG AND SHORT VOWELS

و

This letter doesn't connect to the letter after it

وَ	وُ	وِ
Wa	Wu	We

Short vowels

اوَ	وُو	وِي
Waa	Wuu	Wee

Long vowels

					وَ	وَ

					وُ	وُ

					وِ	وِ

					اوَ	اوَ

					وُو	وُو

					وِي	وِي

حَرْفُ الْيَاء

Yaa'

لَوِّنْ:	Color:

Yad

يَد

Yaa'

يَاء

ي

خَطِّطْ: Trace it:

ي

ي

ي

ي

حَرْفُ الْيَاء

Yaa'

At the end	In the middle	In the beginning
ـي	ـيـ	يـ
كرسِي	بِيت	يَاسْمِين
Korsee	Bayt	Yasmeen

ي

Trace it: خَطِّطْ:

ي

يّ

يِّ

ضَعْ دَائِرَةْ حَوْلْ ٱلْكَلِمَاتْ ٱلتي تَحْتَوِي عَلَى حَرِفْ ٱلـ ي
Circle the words that have the letter Yaa'

دَائِرَة   رَعِد   جَدَتِي

يَمَامَة   بَيْض

بَاب   شَاي

يَقْطِين   أَقْلَام   سَرِير

LONG AND SHORT VOWELS

يَ	يُ	يِ
Ye	Yu	Ya

Short vowels

يَ	يُو	يَا
Yee	Yuu	Yaa

Long vowels

لوِّنْ, واكْتُبْ شَكِلِ الحَرِفْ المُنَاسِبْ لِتَمْلأَ الفَرَاغ

Color and write the correct letter form to fill in the blank

لس	لسـ	ـلس		حـ	ـحـ	ـح

عَــــل

ذَاءْ___

نـ	ـنـ	ـن		كـ	ـكـ	ـك

مـْــل___

عَـ___بوت

بـ	ـبـ	ـب		غـ	ـغـ	ـغ

قَلْ___

ـيْمة___

عـ	ـعـ	ـع		تـ	ـتـ	ـت

نَـ___ب

وت___

لوّنْ, واكْتُبْ شَكِلَ الْحَرِفْ المُناسِبْ لِتَمْلأَ الفَراغ

Color and write the correct letter form to fill in the blank

خ خ خ	هـ ـهـ ـه
صَ___رَة	فَواكِ___

ع أ أ أ	صـ صـ صـ
خُطْبُوط___	مِقَ___

قـ قـ قـ	ضـ ضـ ضـ
___لَم	بَيْ___

نـ نـ نـ	و و
___يْتون	شَمـ___ع

Name:......................

لوّنْ, واكْتُبْ شَكِلْ الحَرِفْ المُنَاسِبْ لِتَمْلَأَ الفَرَاغ

Color and write the correct letter form to fill in the blank

ط ط ط	ف ف ف
بِ___رِيق	___يل
مـ مـ مـ	جـ جـ جـ
___فْتَاح	نَ___مَة
ش ش ش ش	ل ل ل
قِرْ___	سُ___حَفَاة
ذ ذ ذ	ر ر ر
___رَة	شَجَ___ة

Name:.........................

لوّنْ, واكْتُبْ شَكِلْ الحَرِفْ المُنَاسِبْ لِتَمْلَأَ الفَرَاغ

Color and write the correct letter form to fill in the blank

ظ ظ ظ	ثـ ثـ ثـ
نَ__ارَة	___غْبَان
يـ يـ يـ	عـ عـ عـ
___قْطِين	سَا___ة
آ آ	نـ نـ نـ
مِرْ___ة	سِكّيـ___
ة ة	د د
___مُمْحا	قِرْ___

لُوْنُ الدَّوَائِرْ الَّتِي تَحْتَوِي عَلَى نَفْسِ الْكَلِمَةِ بِاللَّوْنِ ذَاتِه.

Color the circles that contain the same word with the same color.

بَ ا لُ و نْ | بَالُون | قَهْوَة | حَ ا سُ و بْ

كُوب | حِ صَ ا نْ | كُ و بْ | فَرَاشَة

شَ ا حِ نَ ة | خِزَانَة | غَ ا بَ ة | شَاحِنَة

غَابَة | حِصَانْ | سُكَرْ | حَاسُوب

سُ كَ رْ | فَ رَ ا شَ ة | قَ هْ وَ ة | خِ زَ ا نَ ة

لُوْنُ الدَّوَائِرْ الَّتِي تَحْتَوِي عَلَى نَفْسِ الْكَلِمَةِ بِاللَّوْنِ ذَاتِهِ.

Color the circles that contain the same word with the same color.

ضَوْءُ	هُدْهُد	حَ دِ ي قَ ة	قِطَارْ
مَطَرْ	دَرَاجَة	تَ ا جْ	مَنْزِلْ
دَرَاجَة	مَ نْ زِ لْ	ضَ وْ ء	حَ جَ ر
حَجَر	طَ بِ ي بْ	قِ طَ ا رْ	هُ دْ هُ د
تَاجْ	حَدِيقة	م َ طَ ر	طَبِيبْ

Answer Keys

Page 16

ضَعْ دَائِرَة حَوْلَ الْكَلِمَاتِ الَّتِي تَحْتَوِي عَلَى حَرْفِ الـ ا
Circle the words that have the letter Alif

قِرْد • أَسَد • وَرْدَة • مُرَبَّع • قَرَأَ • دَجَاجَة • قَهْوَة • بَدَأَ • بَارِد • أَنَانَاس

Page 19

ضَعْ دَائِرَة حَوْلَ الْكَلِمَاتِ الَّتِي تَحْتَوِي عَلَى حَرْفِ الـ ب
Circle the words that have the letter Baa'

أَزْرَق • بَطَّة • مُرَبَّع • دُب • بَقَرَة • هَاتِف • دِيك • أَخْطَبُوط • سَيَّارَة • حَاسُوب

Page 22

ضَعْ دَائِرَة حَوْلَ الْكَلِمَاتِ الَّتِي تَحْتَوِي عَلَى حَرْفِ الـ ت
Circle the words that have the letter Taa'

بَنْك • بَيْت • تَيْس • دُب • تَاج • بِنْت • حُوت • هَاتِف • عَجِين • كُتُب

Page 25

ضَعْ دَائِرَة حَوْلَ الْكَلِمَاتِ الَّتِي تَحْتَوِي عَلَى حَرْفِ الـ ث
Circle the words that have the letter Thaa'

مُثَلَّث • ثَلَاثَة • غَيْث • حُب • دُودَة • مَوْز • ثَوْب • ثَلْج • لَيْث • فِيل

Page 28

ضَعْ دَائِرَة حَوْلَ الْكَلِمَاتِ الَّتِي تَحْتَوِي عَلَى حَرْفِ الـ ج
Circle the words that have the letter Jeem

كُوب • عَجِين • جَبَل • بُرْج • خَرِيف • مَزِيج • قَلْب • رَجُل • جِسْر • نَمِل

Page 31

ضَعْ دَائِرَة حَوْلَ الْكَلِمَاتِ الَّتِي تَحْتَوِي عَلَى حَرْفِ الـ ح
Circle the words that have the letter Haa'

حُبُوب • نَحْلَة • رَبِيع • مَاء • لَحْم • قُبَّعَة • بَلَح • أَسْوَد • حَمَامَة • قَمْح

Page 34

ضَعْ دَائِرَة حَوْلَ الْكَلِمَاتِ الَّتِي تَحْتَوِي عَلَى حَرْفِ الـ خ
Circle the words that have the letter Khaa'

تَارِيخ • حَقِيبَة • مَخْبَز • خَشَب • بَاب • أَصْفَر • خَمْسَة • صَخْرَة • خَوْخ • وَرَقَة

Page 37

ضَعْ دَائِرَة حَوْلَ الْكَلِمَاتِ الَّتِي تَحْتَوِي عَلَى حَرْفِ الـ د
Circle the words that have the letter Dal

دَلْو • بَنَفْسَجِي • مَدْرَسَة • يَد • ضَوْء • أَسَد • صُنْدُوق • دَفْتَر • قَمَر • قَلَم

Page 40

ضَعْ دَائِرَة حَوْلَ الْكَلِمَاتِ الَّتِي تَحْتَوِي عَلَى حَرْفِ الـ ذ
Circle the words that have the letter Thaal

ذِئْب • بُرْتُقَالِي • غِذَاء • جَبَل • عَصِير • جَذَاء • ذَهَب • أُسْتَاذ • تِلْمِيذ • دَرَج

Page 43

ضَعْ دَائِرَة حَوْلَ الْكَلِمَاتِ الَّتِي تَحْتَوِي عَلَى حَرْفِ الـ ر
Circle the words that have the letter Raa'

رَمْل • مَسْبَح • عُشْب • شَعْر • أَرُزّ • هَاتِف • رُمَّان • عَصِير • حَافِلَة • إِبْرِيق

Page 46

ضَعْ دَائِرَة حَوْلَ الْكَلِمَاتِ الَّتِي تَحْتَوِي عَلَى حَرْفِ الـ ز
Circle the words that have the letter Zayn

أَزْرَق • أَرُزّ • حَائِط • بَقَرَة • مِيزَان • أَلْوَان • زَرَافَة • زَهْرَة • مَوْز • طِفْل

Page 49

ضَعْ دَائِرَة حَوْلَ الْكَلِمَاتِ الَّتِي تَحْتَوِي عَلَى حَرْفِ الـ س
Circle the words that have the letter Seen

صَافِي • سَمَاء • مَسْبَح • شَمْس • مَسَاء • دَائِرَة • حَفْلَة • أَوْلَاد • يَابِس • سَلْسَال

Page 52

ضَعْ دَائِرَة حَوْلَ الْكَلِمَاتِ الَّتِي تَحْتَوِي عَلَى حَرْفِ الـ ش
Circle the words that have the letter Sheen

أَرْض • حَرْف • شَعْر • سَطْر • مِشْمِش • قِرَاشَة • حَشَرَة • تِلْفَاز • عُشْ • شَمْس

Page 55

ضَعْ دَائِرَة حَوْلَ الْكَلِمَاتِ الَّتِي تَحْتَوِي عَلَى حَرْفِ الـ ص
Circle the words that have the letter Saad

قُصُور • صُنْدُوق • بَيْت • سَاعَة • نَبَات • إِجَّاص • صَحْرَاء • حَائِط • مِقَص • فُصُول

Page 58

ضَعْ دَائِرَة حَوْلَ الْكَلِمَاتِ الَّتِي تَحْتَوِي عَلَى حَرْفِ الـ ض
Circle the words that have the letter Dhaad

ضِفْدَع • عُلْبَة • عَضَلَة • خَامِض • شَاحِنَة • بَيْضَة • أَسْوَد • ضَبْع • أَبْيَض • زَرَافَة

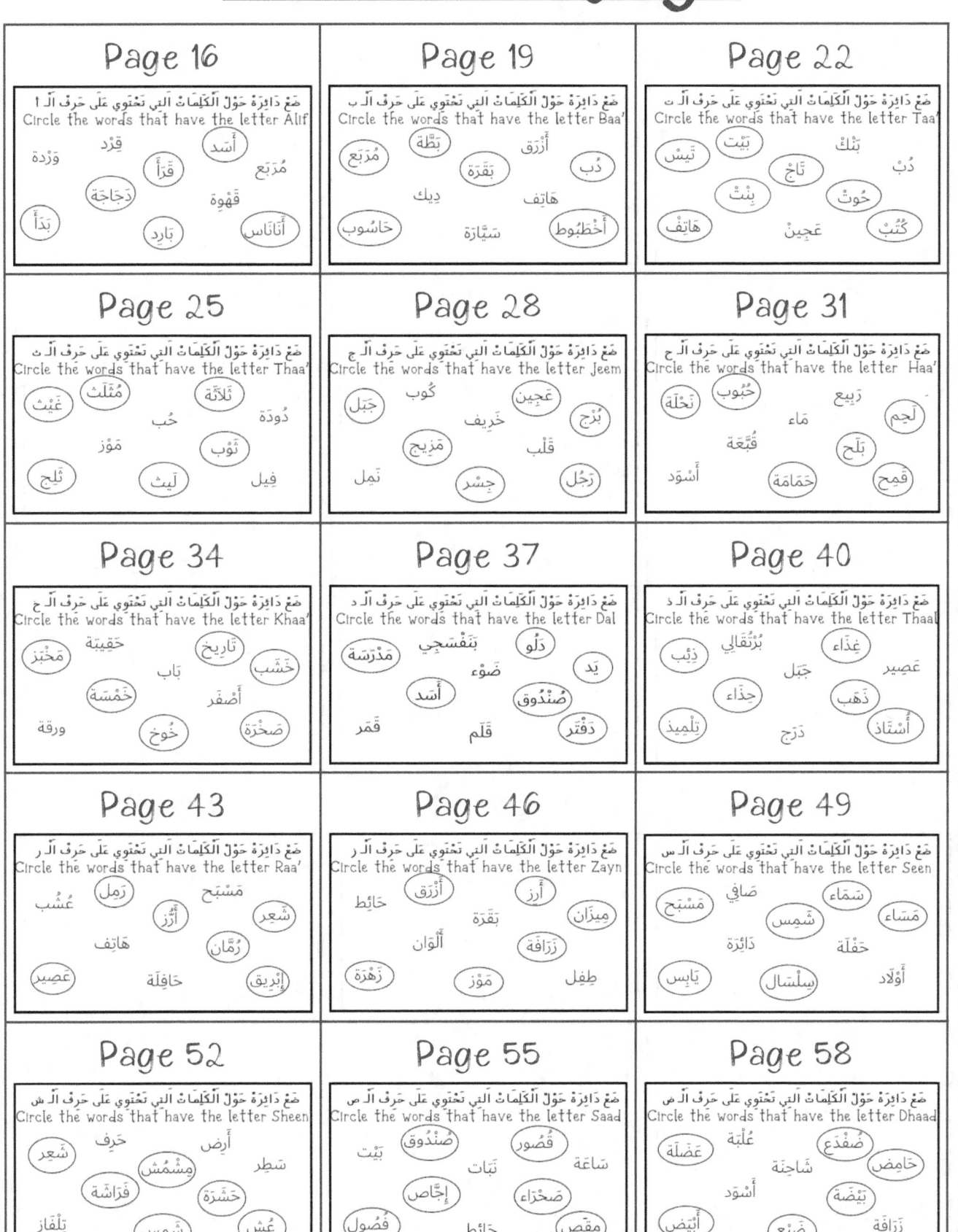

105

Answer Keys

Page 61

ضَعْ دَائِرَة حَوْلَ الْكَلِمَاتِ الَّتِي تَحْتَوِي عَلَى حَرْفِ الْـ ط
Circle the words that have the letter Taa'

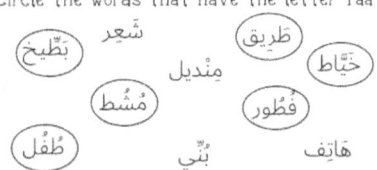

Page 64

ضَعْ دَائِرَة حَوْلَ الْكَلِمَاتِ الَّتِي تَحْتَوِي عَلَى حَرْفِ الْـ ظ
Circle the words that have the letter Zaa'

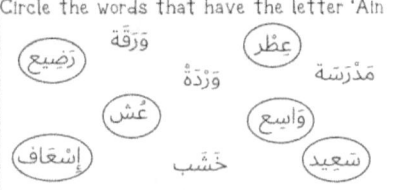

Page 67

ضَعْ دَائِرَة حَوْلَ الْكَلِمَاتِ الَّتِي تَحْتَوِي عَلَى حَرْفِ الْـ ع
Circle the words that have the letter 'Ain

Page 70

ضَعْ دَائِرَة حَوْلَ الْكَلِمَاتِ الَّتِي تَحْتَوِي عَلَى حَرْفِ الْـ غ
Circle the words that have the letter Ghain

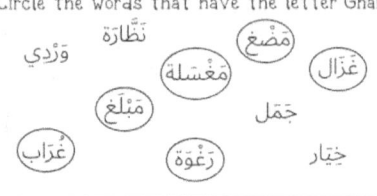

Page 73

ضَعْ دَائِرَة حَوْلَ الْكَلِمَاتِ الَّتِي تَحْتَوِي عَلَى حَرْفِ الْـ ف
Circle the words that have the letter Faa'

Page 76

ضَعْ دَائِرَة حَوْلَ الْكَلِمَاتِ الَّتِي تَحْتَوِي عَلَى حَرْفِ الْـ ق
Circle the words that have the letter Qaaf

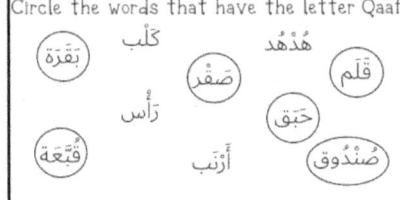

Page 79

ضَعْ دَائِرَة حَوْلَ الْكَلِمَاتِ الَّتِي تَحْتَوِي عَلَى حَرْفِ الْـ ك
Circle the words that have the letter Kaaf

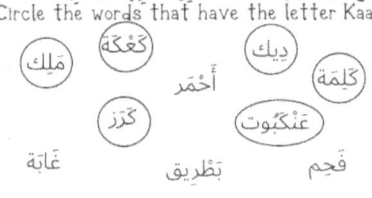

Page 82

ضَعْ دَائِرَة حَوْلَ الْكَلِمَاتِ الَّتِي تَحْتَوِي عَلَى حَرْفِ الْـ ل
Circle the words that have the letter Lam

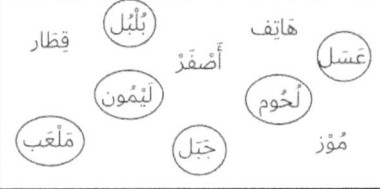

Page 85

ضَعْ دَائِرَة حَوْلَ الْكَلِمَاتِ الَّتِي تَحْتَوِي عَلَى حَرْفِ الْـ م
Circle the words that have the letter Meem

Page 88

ضَعْ دَائِرَة حَوْلَ الْكَلِمَاتِ الَّتِي تَحْتَوِي عَلَى حَرْفِ الْـ ن
Circle the words that have the letter Noon

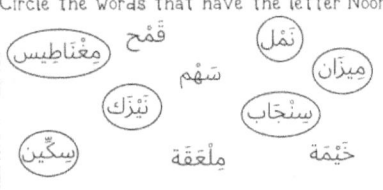

Page 91

ضَعْ دَائِرَة حَوْلَ الْكَلِمَاتِ الَّتِي تَحْتَوِي عَلَى حَرْفِ الْـ ه
Circle the words that have the letter Haa'

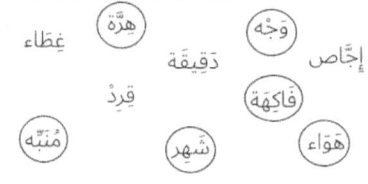

Page 94

ضَعْ دَائِرَة حَوْلَ الْكَلِمَاتِ الَّتِي تَحْتَوِي عَلَى حَرْفِ الْـ و
Circle the words that have the letter Waaw

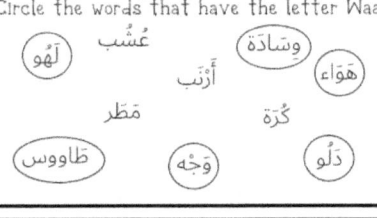

Page 97

ضَعْ دَائِرَة حَوْلَ الْكَلِمَاتِ الَّتِي تَحْتَوِي عَلَى حَرْفِ الْـ ي
Circle the words that have the letter Yaa'

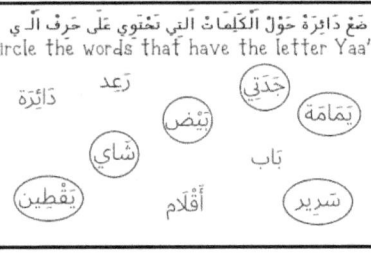

Answer Keys

Page 99

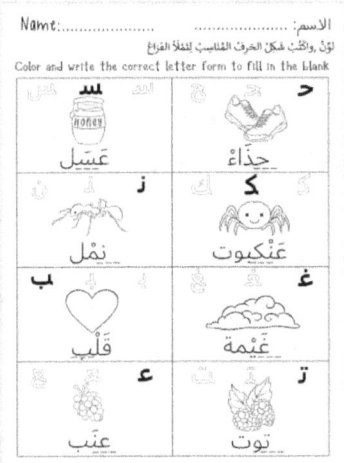

Page 100

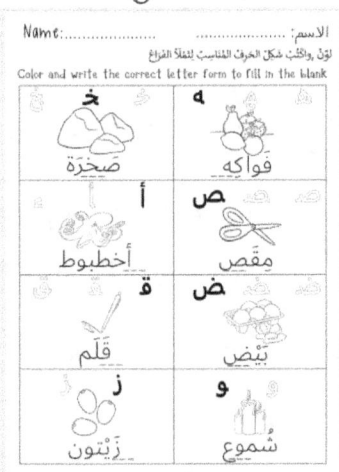

Page 101

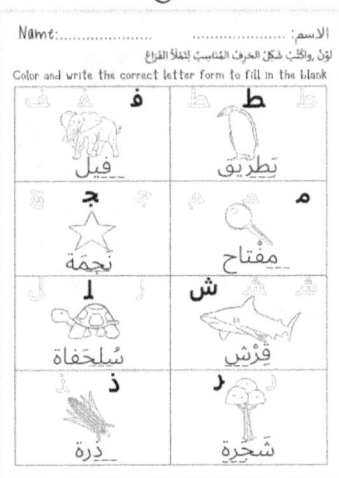

Page 102

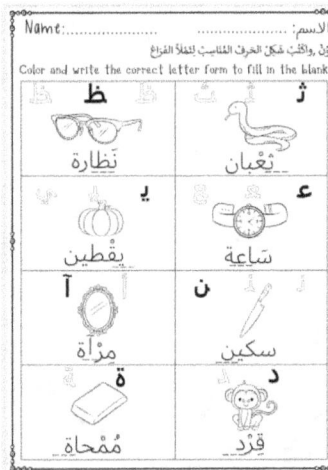

Page 103

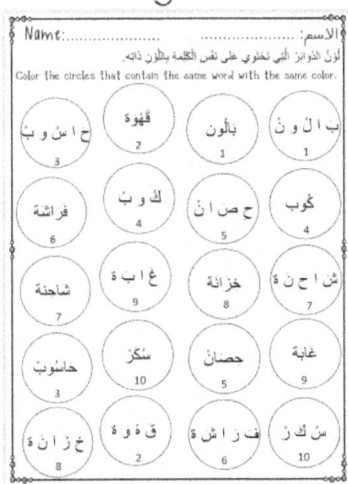

Page 104

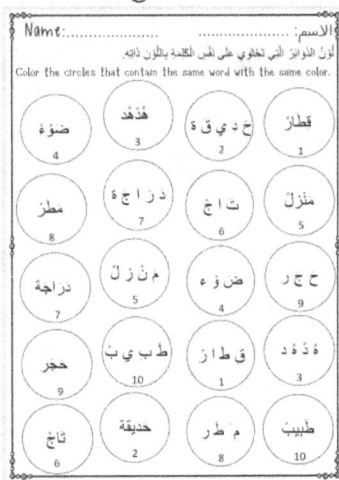

Thank You! ♡

Thank you for choosing this book to learn and explore the Arabic alphabet.

It is our hope that this journey has sparked your curiosity and inspired a love for the Arabic language.

Learning is an adventure, and we are thrilled to be a part of yours.

Keep practicing, stay motivated, and always remember that every step forward is progress!

Your feedback is very important!

If you have a moment, please leave a review of this workbook on Amazon.

Your honest opinion helps other people discover my work.

Thank you for your support!

With heartfelt thanks,
The Author / Abir Kaddouh

شُكْرًا لَكُمْ! ♡

شُكْرًا لِاخْتِيَارِكُمْ هٰذَا ٱلْكِتَابَ لِتَعَلُّمِ وَٱسْتِكْشَافِ ٱلْحُرُوفِ ٱلْعَرَبِيَّةِ.

نَرْجُو أَنْ تَكُونَ هٰذِهِ ٱلرِّحْلَةُ قَدْ أَشْعَلَتْ فُضُولَكُمْ وَأَلْهَمَتْكُمْ حُبَّ ٱللُّغَةِ ٱلْعَرَبِيَّةِ.

ٱلتَّعَلُّمُ هُوَ مُغَامَرَةٌ، وَنَحْنُ مُتَحَمِّسُونَ لِأَنْ نَكُونَ جُزْءًا مِّنْ مُغَامَرَتِكُمْ! ٱسْتَمِرُّوا فِي ٱلْمُمَارَسَةِ، وَٱبْقَوْا مُتَحَفِّزِينَ، وَتَذَكَّرُوا دَائِمًا أَنَّ كُلَّ خُطْوَةٍ إِلَى ٱلْأَمَامِ هِيَ تَقَدُّمٌ.

رَأْيُكُمْ يُهِمُّنِي جِدًّا!

إِذَا كَانَ لَدَيْكُمْ وَقْتٌ، فَرَجَاءً قُومُوا بِكِتَابَةِ تَقْيِيمٍ لِهٰذَا ٱلْكِتَابِ عَلَى مَوْقِعِ أَمَازُون.

رَأْيُكُمُ ٱلصَّادِقُ يُسَاعِدُ ٱلْآخَرِينَ عَلَى ٱكْتِشَافِ أَعْمَالِي.

شُكْرًا جَزِيلًا عَلَى دَعْمِكُمْ!

مَعَ خَالِصِ ٱلشُّكْرِ،
ٱلْمُؤَلِّفَة / عَبِير قَدُّوح